Cheap Thrills

RON GOULART, 1933—

CHEAP THRILLS

An Informal History of the Pulp Magazines

ARLINGTON HOUSE   *New Rochelle, N.Y.*

Library of Congress Catalog Card Number 72-77635

ISBN 0-87000-172-8

MANUFACTURED IN THE UNITED STATES OF AMERICA

Contents

PREFACE

WHEN I began working on this book, something over a year and a half ago, veteran pulp writer W.T. Ballard said to me, "Your big problem will be deciding what to leave out." This turned out to be true. In a book this size, or even twice this size, it isn't possible to talk about all the pulp magazines published in the United States since the 20th century began. Nor about all the daring heroes and underpaid writers. So I have concentrated on giving a general outline of the whole history of the pulp magazines and a more detailed account of one specific period in that history.

The detailed period is that between the two World Wars, roughly from 1920 to 1940. In those years the private eye was born, the masked avengers had one of their periodic flowerings, Lester Dent wrote a hundred whacky novels about Doc Savage, G-8 took to the air with his Battle Aces and Frederick Schiller Faust changed his name to Max Brand. It comes as close as any span of years to being the heyday of the pulp magazine.

Dozens of people, many of them survivors of the pulpwood era, have helped out by providing information, anecdotes, memories and back issues. I thank them all.

CHAPTER ONE

THE PULPWOOD ERA

NOBODY liked Frank A. Munsey. When he died, in 1925, his eulogists said things like, "Frank Munsey contributed to the journalism of his day the talent of a meat packer, the morals of a money changer and the manner of an undertaker." Even the *Dictionary of American Biography* doesn't care much for him. "He was not a reformer, nor an idealist, nor was he deeply interested in any causes," says this biographical source book. "His passion was to found or purchase magazines and, later, newspapers. If one of his magazines failed to earn well he killed it and began another; if public taste passed from one of his productions he dropped it to develop another. . . . He progressed from cheap, inconsequential magazines to more important ones and then to daily newspapers."

But eras and movements, like people, can't pick their

fathers and so a history of the pulp magazines has to begin with the ruthless and unlikable Munsey. It was Frank Munsey who at the end of the 19th century invented the pulpwood fiction magazine. If it had not been for him there might never have been pulps and, consequently, no Tarzan, no Sam Spade, no Dr. Kildare, no Doc Savage, no Zorro, no Shadow and no Tros of Samothrace. Zane Grey might have stayed in dentistry and Charles Atlas might still be a 97-pound-weakling.

What Munsey did was to have an economical notion. A telegraph operator in his home town of Augusta, Maine, Frank Munsey left there for New York in 1882, when he was in his late twenties. He wanted to publish a cheap fiction weekly of inspirational stories for children. Munsey had a difficult time financing the venture but finally, as Frank Luther Mott recounts in his history of American magazines, "the great day came—December 2, 1882— when the first number of the *Golden Argosy, Freighted with Treasures for Boys and Girls* was issued . . . It was an eight-page small-folio containing the opening of a serial by Horatio Alger, entitled 'Do and Dare, or a Brave Boy's Fight for a Fortune,' which began on the front page. Beginning on an inside page was another serial, with the inspiring title 'Nick and Nellie, or God Helps Them That Help Themselves,' by Edward S. Ellis, famous dime-novel author and former editor of *Golden Days* . . . which was really the model for the Munsey venture."

At this point Munsey was in competition with a great many much better established publishers. Weekly story papers had been offering cheap thrills to the American public for almost a half century. "Popular literature on the scale marketed today is as much a product of the Industrial Revolution as is large-scale manufacture of any sort," points out historian Mary Noel. Before the development of steam presses and before the completion of the railroads, printing and distribution of low price magazines was impossible. Says Miss Noel, "In 1830 the United States, with its population of thirteen million, had more so-called newspapers than Europe . . . Such papers, consisting of a huge sheet folded once to make the standard four pages of those early days, provided the cheapest possible format for popular fiction. In the 1830's and early 1840's the United States Post Office added its important encouragement to this format. Without a well-developed system of railroads, there could be no great express system in America and without such a system the retailing of cheap and popular literature through newsstands was an impossibility. . . . The postman himself was America's leading literary agent."

By Munsey's day the printing and distribution of the fiction papers had vastly improved and he also had to worry about competition from the dime novels. These had developed originally as spin-offs of the literary newspapers, but soon turned into a major genre on their own. The publishing firm of Beadle & Adams had tried the books out during the Civil War and soon found themselves among that conflict's major profiteers. The books, according to Miss Noel, "met the requirements of the simple, little-educated men in the Union Army, and by the end of the war Beadle had sold 4,000,000 copies of his dime novels." In 1889, while Frank Munsey was still floundering and was over $20,000 in debt, Street & Smith went into the dime novel business. They had been in the fiction weekly line since the 1850's and they soon found the five- and ten-cent novels were equally profitable.

Munsey meanwhile was having a time one biographer describes as "financially fruitless." He kept modifying his publication. He trimmed the title down to *Argosy* and aimed it at juveniles and adults instead of children. In 1891 he started another magazine, titled *Munsey's*. This was a low priced, illustrated, general audience magazine and it did well, providing Munsey with both money and inspiration. He decided to gain for *Argosy* the kind of general adult audience *Munsey's* was reaching. And at the same time he had that economical notion mentioned above. Cheaper paper. "Tinkering with his *Argosy*," says *Magazines In The Twentieth Century*, "he made it an all-fiction magazine and switched to a rough wood-pulp paper because he thought the story was more important than what it was printed on. Publishers of cheap fiction may have seen that the pulp could save postage. As single publications, dime novels were not eligible for the low second-class postal rates; the pulp magazine was . . ." Munsey's new package for mass fiction was a fat pulp paper magazine with no pictures and the public soon decided they liked buying the stuff that way. *Argosy's* circulation quickly climbed to 80,000 per issue and by the early 1900's the magazine was selling a half-million copies a month. During the first dozen successful years of *Munsey's* and *Argosy*, Frank Munsey not only got out of debt, he earned a net profit of nine million dollars. During the First World War, by which time he'd added *All-Story* and *Cavalier* to his pulp fiction titles, Munsey made *Argosy* a weekly again—something he had been unable to keep it in its first faltering years. Until the Munsey Company introduced *Detective Fiction Weekly* in the 1920's, all the Munsey pulp fiction magazines had been broadly general. Every story category that was later to have pulps of its own appeared in *Argosy*, from love to science fiction with plenty of cowboys, detectives and ape men in between.

Street & Smith followed Munsey into the pulps. They started *Popular Magazine* in 1903, first as a juvenile and then as an imitation of *Argosy*, "stressing action, adventure and the outdoors." *Top-Notch*, another general fiction magazine, followed in 1910. Then Street & Smith got the notion that there might be money in specializing and this resulted in *Detective Story, Western Story, Love*

Story, Sea Stories and *Sport Story.* When this last title showed up, in 1923, the dime novels were long gone and the pulpwood magazine was the dominant format for adventure and romantic fiction. At the close of the First World War there were barely two dozen different pulp titles, but by the middle Depression years over two hundred separate pulps were on sale. Other long-established publishing firms, such as Doubleday and the Butterick Company, had also come into cheap fiction magazines. Doubleday took over *Short Stories* in 1910 and later added a cowboy pulp, *West,* and a mystery and adventure pulp, *Star.* Butterick's chief pulp was *Adventure.* Brand new people set up shop, too, and contributed to the proliferating titles of the years between the wars. A highly successful chain in the '20's was the one founded by William Clayton. Clayton's funds were derived from the earlier impressive sales of a tame girlie magazine called *Snappy Stories.* Jumping to adventure and mystery pulps, Clayton built up a line of a dozen or more titles. An editor who sold him several titles and format ideas–among them *Clues, Ace-High* and *Five Novels*–told me that "before the Depression struck in 1929–30 Clayton had netted several million dollars. Up to that time he was the richest pulp publisher in the business. He went broke in 1932." Included in the magazines Clayton was forced to sell was *Astounding Science Fiction,* which, as *Analog,* is one of the very few pulps to survive into the present.

A publisher who fared better was George T. Delacorte. He founded Dell Publishing in 1922, and is still at it. Delacorte's earliest magazines were pulps, most notably *War Birds.* He also published the Depression humor magazine *Ballyhoo,* and as early as 1929 was experimenting with four-color comic books, a type of cheap magazine that would eventually help kill off the pulps. The Fawcett brothers, Wilford and Roscoe, also went into pulpwood magazines. But their pulps never did as well as such other

Fawcett magazines as *Captain Billy's Whiz-Bang, Captain Marvel Comics* and *True.* Aaron A. Wyn, described as "a strapping six-footer, newshawk on the Pacific coast, school teacher in Idaho, cowhand in Wyoming and able seaman," built his Ace Publishing Company on pulps. Ned L. Pines, who started the Popular Library paperback house, had one of the largest pulp lines of the 1930's. He started in the magazine field in 1927, with a periodical called *College Life.* "In 1930 Street & Smith, one of the best customers of the American News Company, left that organization to have its publications independently distributed," explains Frank L. Schick in *The Paperbound Book in America.* "Ned Pines was asked to fill the gap created by this withdrawal. He launched a number of fiction magazines." Helping Pines with the launching was his long-time friend Leo Margulies, veteran of assorted Munsey enterprises. The two young men brought out numerous pulps, including *The Phantom Detective.* Their magazines sold for ten cents and were meant to compete with and undersell the Street & Smith pulps on the Depression newsstands. The Depression created another mammoth dispenser of cheap thrills, Popular Publications. Founded by Henry Steeger and Harold S. Goldsmith in the early Thirties, the Popular house featured "Dime" in the titles of their first magazines—*Dime Detective, Dime Sports, Dime Adventures*—usually Street & Smith's generic titles with a cheaper price stuck in front. Popular prospered, eventually buying out a good many of its competitors.

A standard pulp magazine format had been arrived at by the 1920's and most of the houses conformed to it. The average pulp consisted of 128 rough-edged pulpwood paper pages and had a cover of more expensive, coated stock. The cover served as a package and an advertisement and so it was both bright and provocative. Basic colors and intense action prevailed. Sales appeal was more important than art, and one cover painter remembers being told that all the covers he did for a certain Western pulp had to be predominantly yellow, because yellow sold well off the stands. He painted several dozen yellow cowboy covers. The interiors of the pulps were, visually, a letdown, and you had to actually read the stories to get anywhere near the thrills promised by the cover. Later comic books, somewhat like buffered aspirin, cut down the time it took for the action to get from the page to the brain—and they took away much of the pulps' audience. Sometime after World War I, illustrators like Frank Hoffman took to doing illustrations for the slick magazines using India ink and water color brushes. This black and white dry-brush technique, as perfected by Hoffman, "inspired countless imitators among the pulp magazine illustrators, who found the technique ideally suited to reproduction in line," according to art historian Walt Reed. Though a lot of pulp illustration was hurried or inept, there were quite a few good men illustrating for the pulpwoods in the 1920's and 1930's. For a brief period even Rockwell Kent's stark black and white spots showed up in pulps, in the pages of *Adventure.*

The older Munsey pulps had run as many as four serials per issue, but by the anxious '20's the continued story was diminishing in popularity and the most an editor would dare offer the impatient public of the jazz age was one serial. Often, magazines tried to give the impression that the continuing episodes of a novel were really just short stories that happened to feature the same characters all the time. As a rule, a pulp magazine ran about a half dozen short stories and one or two longer pieces of fiction. The term Complete Novel was applied, depending on the integrity of the publisher and the supposed gullibility of the readers, to everything from an 8,000-word short story to a real novel ten times that long.

In addition to roughly 200,000 words of fiction, most

pulps offered their customers all manner of short features. The letter column was the most frequent filler. A good part of the letters always sounded, no matter what the decade, like this one Gilbert G. Hale of Worcester, Massachusetts sent to *All-Story* in 1916:

> To the Editor:
>   Over a year ago, while spending a vacation at Bustin's Island, Casco Bay, Maine, I picked up one of your magazines, intending to pass away a few moments of spare time, and ever since reading that copy I have been an ardent enthusiast.

Frequently readers were in a more technical-minded mood:

> The front cover of the April 30 issue shows the left fore-arm, right hand and bow and arrow of what is apparently an American Indian archer. Now, what I want to know is, did any one ever know of an Indian using the method of arrow release employed by the archer in this picture?

And, just as frequently, eager to help out the editors:

> Sirs:
>   I've just finished the July *AMAZING STORIES* and here's my rating on the stories:
>   1. *Gods of the Jungle*—the best serial in a long time!
>   2. *The Return of Hawk Carse*—how about a sequel?
>   3. *Squadron of the Damned*—make O'Brien continue this thrilling story!
>   4. *The World Beyond*—Cummings is always writing about a new Utopia!
>   5. *The Powers of Darkness*—Swain is a master of suspense!
>   Here's my rating of the illustrations . . .

Clubs and services abounded during the pulp's golden age. You could join the Doc Savage Club, the War Birds Flying Club, the Ends-of-the-Earth Club, the Spider League for Crime Prevention, the Friends of the Phantom and dozens more. Even the American Legion, as we'll see in a later chapter, began as a pulp magazine club. Several pulps ran information services for readers, the largest-scale operation being "Ask *Adventure*." This section gave the curious reader half a hundred experts or more whom he could query directly. Topics covered included Camping and Woodcraft, Tropical Forestry, Taxidermy, Aviation, Asia and the Sea. Vast topics such as the Sea, were divided into parts. For American Waters information you had to contact Lt. Harry E. Riesenberg of Alexandria, Va. For British Waters you got in touch with Captain Dingle. *Adventure* carried, as did many of the cowboy pulps, a missing persons service for readers. Theirs was called "Lost Trails" and printed pages of small type, often sad, items such as:

Dutch. Please write to your old pal.

Romans, Donald L. Last heard of in Los Angeles, in 1921. Please write to your mother or me.

Conrad, Ira L. Known as "Silvers." U.S.M.C., 1907. Last seen in Milwaukee, Wis., 1907, working as molder for Filer & Stoddard Foundry Co. His one time pal and friend William R. Bethel would like to hear from him.

Also sandwiched in with the stories were puzzle and problem-solving features. *Detective Fiction Weekly,* for instance, offered "Solving Cipher Secrets" by M.E. Ohaver, a code-breaking section filled with challenging messages like: UNG CPGBUN TK UNG ATPRORL, etc.

The pulpwood magazines also involved their readers in the world of advertising. Usually small space, one column

by an inch or two, the pulp advertisers offered such things
as health and well-being:

BURNING FEET
Ended In 3 Seconds

Bladder Sufferers Make FREE Test

Ruptured?

Correct Your Nose!!

Defer Life's Afternoon
With REJUVI-MATE

4 Inches Of Muscle Put
On Your Arms

Another commodity was money:

Find GOLD!

I'll Fill your pocketbook
and Give You a Brand New
Ford Tudor Sedan

We Will Pay $500
Just for a Baby's Name

And, particularly during the Depression, the need of a job
was exploited:

Do You Want a U.S. GOV'T.
Position?

Earn Money At Home

Be A Railway Traffic Inspector

Learn Electricity

Big Money Selling Shirts

Sex sold well, too:

Lonely?

Female Beauty Round The World
World's Greatest Collection of
Strange and Secret Photographs

What Compelling POWERS Did the
Great Lovers of History POSSESS?

Illustrated Booklets & Novelties
The Kind Men Like!

The pulps sold fountain pens, contraceptives, hamsters, false teeth, giant toads, radios, eyeglasses, education, ventriloquism secrets and Tillie & Mac comic booklets.

But they also sold heroes.

CHAPTER TWO

HEROES FOR SALE

For our purposes it is sufficient to define a hero as a human figure—real or imaginary or both—who has shown greatness in some achievement.

—Daniel J. Boorstin,
The Image

A good many of the products of popular culture have always been generated by the preoccupations and anxieties of children and adolescents. This means that the mass entertainments of any period will invariably be much concerned with action and identity. Speaking about school age children, Dr. Benjamin Spock says, "They delight in stories in which good is pitted against evil and always wins in the end. And since this is the stage when they feel from within the necessity to bottle up and control their aggressive impulses in daily life, there is all the more reason to dream of bold adventures and violent battles."

As kids move through the precarious territory between childhood and adolescence their absorption with roles and occupations grows. "They are sometimes morbidly, often curiously, preoccupied with what they appear to be in the eyes of others as compared with what they feel they are," writes Erik Erikson of young people in their later school years, "and with the question of how to connect the roles and skills cultivated earlier with the ideal proto-types of the day." Popular entertainment that is going to appeal to youth, then, has to offer both distractions from and simplified solutions to some of the problems involved in getting from ten to twenty. One basic cultural product that offers both action and alternate identity is the fictional hero.

As was noted in the previous chapter, the pulps had many predecessors in the low-price heroics field. A quick look at some of the predecessors of the pulp heroes is pertinent at this early point in our history. Heroes had begun to become increasingly accessible back in the 19th century. From the early 1800's on, the people in America grew more literate and printing grew faster and cheaper. As the century progressed, more and more people were able to, and wanted to, read about famous men—politicians, soldiers and celebrities. The word *celebrity* was first used as a noun in the 1850's, when improvements in communications were making it much easier to be well-known. Besides real heroes, the unfolding 19th century offered a growing number of made-up heroes, and quite a few, like Daniel Boone, Davy Crockett, Kit Carson and Buffalo Bill, who were partly real and a good deal ficti-tious. Magazines blossomed. You could now subscribe to them for next to nothing. Cheap books became abundant, and heroes multiplied until the end of the century—Old Sleuth, Frank Reade, Jr, Nick Carter, Frank Merriwell,

Deadwood Dick and even Roaring Ralph Rockwood the Ruthless Ranger.

The Wild West, destined to be one of the staples of the pulps, was invented before the cowboy. The first western heroes were the trailblazers, hunters, scouts. In talking of the middle of the 19th century, of the time when the Wild West became a popular literature subject, Professor Henry Nash Smith says, "For Americans of that period there were two quite distinct Wests: the commonplace domesticated area within the agricultural frontier, and the Wild West beyond it. The agricultural West was tedious; its inhabitants belonged to a despised social class. The Wild West was by contrast an exhilarating region of adventure and comradeship in the open air." Daniel Boone was one of the earliest real wilderness men to be turned into a fictional hero.

Then came Kit Carson. Mountain man and scout Kit Carson, according to Smith, "owed his fame to Jessie Benton Fremont's skillful editing of her husband's reports of his exploring in the early 1840's. Although these narratives had been widely read before 1846, the Mexican War created an even greater audience for them by bringing to bear on everything related to the winning of the West the yeasty nationalism aroused by the conflict." Kit Carson's eminence coincided with the development of the weekly story papers and he was soon fitted into the pattern required by steam literature. The Carson character appeared in story paper serials and dime novels in such adventures as *Kit Carson, The Prince of the Gold Hunters* and *The Fighting Trapper; Or, Kit Carson To The Rescue.* He is written of as a renowned Indian fighter, daredevil horseman, slayer of wild animals. He is a loner, self-contained in a vast savage wilderness.

The Wild West story now began to proliferate in the fiction papers and five and dime novels. Characters named Seth Jones, Nick Whiffles, and Kent the Ranger appear. And, in the words of Henry Nash Smith, "the outworn formulas had to be given zest by constant search after novel sensations. Circus tricks of horsemanship, incredible feats of shooting, more and more elaborate costumes, masks and passwords were introduced." In the 1860's and '70's, such heroes as Mustang Sam, who wore a velvet and silk costume, and Moccasin Mat, a former Texas Ranger with a mighty horse called Storm Cloud, appeared.

In 1869, the best remembered of the semi-real wild westerners made his fiction debut. During Christmas week of that year a serial titled *Buffalo Bill, the King of the Border Men* began running in Street & Smith's *New York Weekly*. The adventure was the work of Col. Ned Buntline, the pen name of a long-time hack named Edward Z.C. Judson. Buntline had been in the cheap fiction trade since the late 1830's and was the author of such works as *The Black Avenger of the Spanish Main; Or, the Fiend of Blood* and *The Red Revenger; Or, the Pirate King of the Floridas.* He had also ghosted political tracts and had bumped into William F. Cody while at Fort McPherson, Nebraska. Buntline was there trying to persuade a well-known Indian scout to let himself be fictionalized, but the man refused and sent Buntline to talk to the young and obscure Cody, who had already hunted down and killed enough buffalo to earn the nickname Buffalo Bill. Cody appears to have needed money and he entered into partnership with Buntline. Numerous serials and novels followed as well as Wild West shows and theatricals. Col. Buntline is said to have made upwards of $20,000 by turning Wm. F. Cody into a property. When Buffalo Bill and his first biographer argued over profits, Cody fired Buntline and hired Colonel Prentiss Ingraham. The saga continued for the rest of the century and into the 20th.

Another highly successful Wild West hero of the late 19th century was Deadwood Dick. His adventures were

written by Edward L. Wheeler and he appeared in a series of Beadle Company dime novels. Wheeler, who had
never been in the west, was fond of alliterative titles.
Deadwood Dick at Danger Divide, *Deadwood Dick's Dia-
monds*, etc. Dick, who took his name from the mining
town in the Dakota Territory, was not a scout or a trapper.
He is, in the majority of his adventures, a freelance, a
man of independent income who travels the Wild West.
He is accompanied by his coterie and they delight in
righting wrongs. Wheeler's novels also introduced
Calamity Jane, who wore men's clothes—including a
jacket with ten-dollar gold pieces for buttons and a belt of
self-cocking five-shooters. Wheeler spoke of Calamity
and Dick as "two wild spirits who have learned each
other's faults and each other's worth, in lives branded
with commingled shame and honor."

Wild West heroes continued into the 20th century.
Some, as we'll see later, turned into pulp heroes. One of
the later of the Buffalo Bill-Deadwood Dick types to appear was Young Wild West. He showed up in the *Wild
West Weekly*, which began in 1902. Each week he was
featured in a thirty-thousand-word novel attributed to An
Old Scout. Some of his adventures were *Young Wild West,
the Lasso King; or, The Crooked Gang of 'Straight' Ranch*
and *Young Wild West, in the Grand Canyon; or, A Finish
Fight with Outlaws*. Old Scout often described his hero as
"a dashing-looking young horseman with flowing light
chestnut hair. Attired in a fancy hunting suit of buckskin,
trimmed elaborately with scarlet silk fringe, and seated
on the back of a splendid sorrel stallion, he made a true
picture of a Western hero." Young Wild West, also known
as the Champion Deadshot of the West and the Prince of
the Saddle, was also a freelance adventurer. He and his
sidekicks owned mine stock and "could well afford to pur-
sue their favorite hobby, which was traveling about the
country on horseback in search of adventure and what-

ever fortune they might chance to come across." Young Wild West's circle included an old scout called Cheyenne Charlie, a young man named Jim Dart, two Chinese servants and an assortment of sweethearts. Young Wild West, who survived into the late 1920's, is still something of the gentleman out west. But the real cowboy was on the horizon and he was to flourish in the pulps.

Gilbert Patten and his wife and son were living modestly in Maine when Street & Smith asked him to create Frank Merriwell, a versatile and athletic hero who would influence a whole generation of pulp writers. Patten, then in his late twenties, had been writing for the fiction weeklies and dime novels since he was sixteen. The dime novel had begun to fade as the end of the 19th century approached and, as one historian puts it, "Street & Smith were alert to changing times. For a year or more they had detected a gradual falling off in demand for the five-cent weeklies. The Wild West type was notably fading. Of the detectives, only Nick Carter was holding fast. It was patently time for a new series, or library as they were known." Ormond Smith, a second generation Smith, asked Patten to try a series about a schoolboy hero, whose life was filled not only with the academic but with adventure and athletics.

This hero, christened with the open and healthy name of Frank Merriwell, was to be upper middle class so he could afford both college and adventure. He was to have, Smith suggested to Patten, a circle that included a Dutchman, an Irishman and a character with "any other dialect you are familiar with." The stories were to be signed Burt L. Standish and, after a dozen or so episodes at prep school, Frank Merriwell was to go on to Yale. Not a college man himself, Patten's closest connection with Yale up to then was when a melodrama of his folded in New Haven. But, like many pulp writers to come, he was able to fake it. Frank Merriwell made his debut in the *Tip Top*

Weekly in 1896 and was for more than two decades the best known Yale man in the world. Not that there had been a lack of school and college boy heroes before Merriwell, but they didn't fit the 1890's as well as he did. Blood and thunder was still important, though some new notions of what a hero should be were even more important. What Street & Smith had brought forth in Frank Merriwell was, as Stewart Holbrook points out in his account of the Merriwell career, "the authentic, patented, All-American youth—gentlemanly, educated, adventurous, brave, handsome, brilliant, athletic, healthy, and almost unbearably clean-living." New ambitions and standards were affecting the public as the new century approached and it showed in the kind of heroes they wanted.

Detectives seem not to have become abundant as fictional heroes until relatively late in the 19th century. Poe's stories of Dupin had appeared in 1841 and did not start much of a trend. The detective novels of the Frenchman Gaboriau, written in the 1860's, were widely pirated in America as were those of Dickens and Wilkie Collins. *Bleak House*, published in 1852, briefly features Inspector Bucket, the first detective to appear in British fiction. Collins' books, such as *The Moonstone*, of 1868, also made use of professional detectives.

It is likely that the activities and memoirs of Alan Pinkerton and the private detective agency he founded in 1850 were also influences on the development of cheap fiction detective stories in the United States. Pinkerton eventually gathered some of his cases in a book and this case book was issued with the Pinkerton slogan "We Never Sleep" and his wide-open eye trademark on the cover. Other case books followed. By the 1880's the story paper publishers were issuing libraries about a number of sleuths and investigators. Old Cap Collier, Old King Brady and Old Sleuth. Old Sleuth had first appeared in the *Fireside Companion* in 1872. Of this type of detective,

Mary Noel says, "The detective stories of the publications made no fundamental change in either characterization or plot. They simply substituted a detective for some other man or hero. The detective went right on rescuing heroines from their abductors." The increasing popularity of Old Sleuth and similar detectives, Mary Noel attributes as much to an urban setting for the stories as to their plots. "The detective was perfectly adapted to the confused traffic and bewildering ways of the rapidly growing city."

One of the hardiest of 19th-century detectives was Nick Carter, a Street & Smith product. He made his bow in a cameo part in their *New York Weekly* in the Fall of 1886 in a story entitled *The Old Detective's Pupil; or, The Mysterious Crime of Madison Square.* He soon became the top banana with a series of his own. The creator of the famous master sleuth was John Coryell, a relative of one of the Smiths. When Coryell was promoted to writing love stories, the company looked for a new writer to take over. "Nick Carter might have suffered the fate of many other short-lived Street & Smith heroes if Frederick Marmaduke Van Rensselaer Dey had not happened on the scene," Robert Clurman tells us in his introduction to *Nick Carter, Detective.* "One day in 1889, Ormond Smith and his brother George had lunch with Dey. They told him they thought the Nick Carter stories had possibilities and they were looking for someone to do a full-fledged series. Dey was a different personality from Coryell . . . But in his quiet, diffident way he convinced the Smith brothers that he could handle the Nick Carter series . . . and for seventeen years thereafter, Dey turned out Nick Carter stories virtually at the rate of one a week."

Like Frank Merriwell, Nick Carter was clean-cut and impressively strong. Though he did much clue-gathering and trail-following, he appealed to boy readers not as much for his ratiocinations as for his derring-do. He

could box, fence, swim and operate whatever new mechanism came along—automobiles, airplanes, etc. And, as
the logo on the 1890's *Nick Carter Weekly* indicated, he
was a master at appearing in various disguises. In his
study of boys' fiction, E.S. Turner observes, "Nick Carter
went to great pains when disguising himself. He would
cheerfully run the clippers over his hair, stain his teeth,
and torture his ears with gold wire. And when he became
a hunchback—his strong line—he was not content with a
hump which came away when he removed his coat (as
some operators apparently were): the hump lay 'deeper
than the coat or the flowered waistcoat that covered it. It
was deeper than the shirt beneath the heavy, coarse woollen undershirt he wore, in fact, so that if occasion should
arise to remove his coat, as was likely to happen, the
hump was still there.' Even when he took the last garment from his back you had difficulty in spotting that the
hump was a dummy. When not in use the hump was kept
in a cupboard and must have baffled the housekeeper
when she came round tidying up." With his props and
stunts, Nick Carter helped make the detective a popular
cheap fiction character. He had a pulp career, which will
be covered later, and as a paperback spy known as the
Killmaster, he is still with us.

Building on the story paper and dime novel background
and on these basic types, the pulp magazines became,
particularly in the decades between the two World Wars,
one of the major packagers of fiction heroes. There was
competition, from the movies and from radio, but until
the 1940's the pulps were the best cheap source of thrills
and heroics. And while the pulp audience was by no
means limited to juveniles, it is safe to say that without
the schoolboy reader the pulps would never have flourished as they did. Hundreds of different pulpwood paper
magazines came into being from 1920 on and they offered
every possible kind of hero. The pulps sold cowboys, de-

tectives, lumberjacks, spies, Royal Canadian Mounted Policemen, sandhogs, explorers, ape men, aviators, phantoms, robots, talking gorillas, boxers, G-men, doughboys, spacemen, Foreign Legionaires, knights, crusaders, corsairs, reporters, Masked Marvels, ballplayers, doctors, playboys, pirates, kings, stuntmen, cops, commandos and magicians—usually for ten cents and never for more than twenty-five cents.

CHAPTER THREE

SOLDIERS OF FORTUNE, ETC.

To be a member, a man must possess the staunch heart of an adventurer, tried and tested on the far-flung out-trails, or have a real desire to be one.

Members of the A.E.F., and Allied Armies, the Foreign Legion, the Army, Navy or Marine Corps, the Aviation Service—all are eligible for the ranks of the *World Adventurers'* clan. Others must prove they are adventurers of the real stripe. If you've undergone some grueling experience, hunted thrills in distant climes, been close to the horrors of shipwreck, railroaded, stalked game, explored beyond the mast, ridden behind the "joy stick"—in fact, rubbed shoulders with danger in any form—you're entitled to enroll in the Brotherhood of He-Men.

To apply for membership, fill out the coupon below.

—Action Stories

FOR quite a while pulp heroes were sold in bunches. The magazines that followed *Argosy* and *All-Story* into the slowly burgeoning pulpwood field emulated Munsey's eclectic approach. So *Adventure*, *Short Stories*, *Blue Book*, *Popular*, *Top-Notch* and *People's* presented readers with a mixed bag of heroics each issue. One cowboy, one explorer, one legionaire, one pirate and two or three musketeers. Most of them succeeded with this liberal format and continued with it throughout the reign of the pulps.

In 1891 Trumbull White explored North Western Ontario in a canoe with his wife. And that was only one of the adventuresome things he did before he became the first editor of *Adventure* magazine in 1910. In 1896, for example, White and his wife bicycled across America and wrote about it for *Outing*. Cycling was not only more popular then, it was much more dangerous. Four years earlier a man named Frank G. Lenz had begun a series for *Outing* magazine covering his trip around the world on a bike. Lenz got no further than Kurdistan, where the natives killed him. Trumbull White survived his canoe and bicycle adventures and went on to investigate the Canadian gold fields, make inquiries into business conditions in Mexico and serve as a news correspondent in Cuba during the Spanish-American War. He then hit Hawaii, Samoa, New Zealand, Central Asia and Siberia. After the turn of the century White slowed down some and, except for an occasional trip by steamer to Europe or a quick jaunt to Alaska, devoted himself to magazine editing. Before starting *Adventure* he'd edited *Red Book*. The publishers of *Adventure* didn't share White's intrepid background, having made their first fortune in the ladies' dress pattern business. The Ridgway Company listed as publisher of the new monthly was a subsidiary of the Butterick Company, founded a half century before by a Boston tailor named Ebenezer Butterick. At the time *Adventure* first appeared, late in 1910, the Butterick organization was one of the largest American magazine publishers and had among its thirty some periodicals the popular mass magazine with the perfect mass title, *Everybody's*, and the fashion-oriented *Delineator*. The restless Trumbull White left the new pulp before it was a year old and went on to other magazines and explorations. *Adventure* has survived, though in increasingly shabby form, to the present. At its best it was thought of as the aristocrat of the cheap magazines, the *Atlantic Monthly* of the pulps. It published everyone from H. Rider Haggard to George Jean Nathan, inspired a pack of imitators, and is probably the only pulp to have one of its former associate editors win the Nobel Prize for Literature.

The next editor after Trumbull White stayed on the job for sixteen years. This was Arthur Sullivant Hoffman, who'd worked as managing editor on the *Delineator* and as assistant to White. Hoffman was in his middle thirties, a "lank, bushy eye-browed young man." He'd made Phi Beta Kappa at Ohio State and done graduate work in English at the University of Chicago. Talking of the magazine's early days many years later, Hoffman said, "It had to struggle against the feeling of both the critics and the general public that no action story could be literary. This is, of course, absurd. If action, however violent, evolves from character, there is no higher literary expression and the ultimate crystallization of character is likely to be physical rather than psychological action." During Hoffman's decade and a half of editorship *Adventure* printed somewhere between 50 million and 100 million words of fiction. By the mid 1920's, when the now successful magazine was coming out every ten days, *Adventure* provided its readers with a half million words each month. Whether or not any of this great mountain of words was literature, as Hoffman believed, a substantial portion of it was high quality escape fiction.

Not content with merely picking stories, Hoffman rumbled through the whole magazine, inventing features, selecting artwork, arguing with readers, starting clubs. Hoffman talked directly to his readers more than probably any other pulp editor. In May of 1912 he initiated a letter section, The Camp-Fire, "a Meeting Place for Readers, Writers and Adventurers." Unlike many later, and feebler, Letters To The Editor sections, in The Camp-Fire the editor himself did a good part of the talking. He talked about anti-gun laws—"If only the advocates of the national anti-revolver law would stop considering theories only and look at the cold, hard facts, they'd cease to be advocates." He talked about aid to the American Indians —"We are being called on to help the suffering people of a long list of nations, of Christian, Jewish, Greek and Mohammedan or of no faith at all. Well and good, but charity begins at home." He talked about participatory government—"For some fourteen years I've been pounding away on the fact that our country can not escape from her ever increasing political, economic and sociological evils until the individual citizens at least approximate meeting an individual citizen's duty and obligation under a democracy—until they take an active and honest hand in public affairs." He talked about the authors, artwork and makeup of the magazine—"Also thought it was about time to unify and renew the little 'dingbats' that run in the text. So far as I know, *Adventure* was the first magazine to use dingbats in this way, though others have since copied the idea from us. Our collection of them was gathered during the years, the work of many different artists." Hoffman also added the "Ask Adventure" and "Lost Trails" sections and a folk song research section called "Old Songs That Men Have Sung."

Adventure ran serials, novelets, short stories, complete novels and some ballad poetry. Hoffman gave considerable space in The Camp-Fire to material by and about his authors, whom he liked to call his Writers' Brigade. He had a cadre of editorial assistants. The most notable among them was Sinclair Lewis. Lewis, later to turn down the Pulitzer Prize but accept the Nobel, worked for Hoffman in the years prior to World War I. His biographer, Marc Schorer, tells us, "The old Butterick Building was a huge pile, with presses in the basements and many floors of packaging and mailing rooms. The main lobby of the editorial suite was elaborate with stained glass, leaded panes, dark-wood paneling, and old Mr. Gannon, one of the company officers, is reported often to have remarked that it looked like a 'fifty-dollar house,' an impression that was heightened by the scores of underpaid young girls who worked there. In this atmosphere of vulgar opulence, Hoffman and Lewis put together their unlikely magazine . . . Lewis and Hoffman shared the job of reading manuscripts, copy editing, correcting proof, setting up dummies, and every other bit of routine that the publishing of a magazine involves, and the relationship between them was always amicable." Lewis probably had a hand in the founding of some of Hoffman's departments and clubs. While he was with the magazine the Adventurers' Club was started and shortly after he left Hoffman came up with the idea for the American Legion. The official American Legion histories downplay Hoffman's connection with the group as we know it, but admit that most of the founders of the real Legion belonged to the earlier version Hoffman began by way of the editorial pages of *Adventure*. Hoffman's Legion was born in 1914 when United States involvement in a world war seemed inevitable. According to one history of the Legion, "the idea, elaborated by Hoffman and by some of his readers, was for all former soldiers, sailors and marines of the United States to get organized so as to be ready to serve their country when needed. General Leonard Wood had encouraged the idea, Theodore Roosevelt had endorsed it."

Despite all the sidelines, Hoffman's first love was adventure fiction. Among the many who early joined his Writers' Brigade was Harold Lamb, who wrote a great number of novelets about Klit the Cossack. These stories of exotic adventure and rough fighting were set in 16th century Russia and Central Asia and are full of the saber clashes and wine guzzling that delighted not only pulp readers but the lonely and ill young Harold Lamb. He had done all his research for these tales in the library at Columbia University, while working full time on a motor trade weekly. To Lamb, Hoffman was an "understanding editor, who allowed me to write anything I wanted." The Klit stories had such titles as "The Mighty Manslayer," "The Star Of Evil Omen," and "The Bride Of Jagannath." They would begin: "It was the year of the lion at the very end of the sixteenth century when Klit guided his horse into Astrakan," or "The heavy morning dew lay on the grass of the Land of the Five Rivers, the Punjab." There was much hard riding and fighting.

Talbot Mundy, another frequent contributor to *Adventure*, was a contrast to Lamb. The writers for Hoffman's magazine were evenly divided between those who researched and imagined and those who had been there and recorded. Given a certain amount of talent, either method was productive of effective adventure fiction. Mundy's had been an active, world traveller's life. Writing in the third person, he once gave this account of himself: "Talbot Mundy was born in London and educated at Rugby. After spending a year in Germany, studying agriculture, he had a Government job at Baroda in India and subsequently wandered all over India on horseback, even penetrating Tibet. Fascinated by the Indian occult teachings, he neglected no opportunity to learn all he could about them . . . Mundy's subsequent wanderings include Australia and the whole length and breadth of Africa. For a considerable time he was in Government

service in the country now known as Kenya, where he
mastered several of the native languages. While in
Africa, he did a great deal of big game hunting; but
his chief interest was native magic, which he studied
intensively . . . Mundy took out first papers in 1911
soon after reaching the United States, where he became a citizen in 1917." He sold his first story to *Adventure* in 1911, the first year he was in America.
Though he also sold to such slick paper markets as
The Saturday Evening Post and *McClure's*, Mundy's
best remembered work was done for *Adventure*.
Mundy had too similar a background to escape the
Kipling influence and some of his early work is in that
vein. In 1925 he wrote the first of many Tros of Samothrace novels for Hoffman's magazine. These wan-
dering, anachronistic, brawling and slightly goofy stories of the prodigious freelance pirate, Tros, are more
representative of Mundy's rambling life and jigsaw er-
udition. The Tros cycle is built up of bits of Roman
Britain history, sea lore, ancient sorceries, Arthurian
legends from several centuries later, Cleopatra myths,
home-made epigrams, saloon fights, practical jokes,
high romance and even a little theosophy (to which
Mundy was partial). The novels anticipate Robert E.
Howard's heavy-handed Conan epics, the Technicolor
phase of Cecil B. DeMille and a little of *A Funny
Thing Happened On The Way To The Forum*. Mundy
invented James Grim, the gentleman agent better
known as Jimgrim, for *Adventure*, too. Starting in
1921, the Jimgrim stories, taking place in various loca-
tions in the mysterious East, showed up regularly.
Grim seems to have been suggested by Lawrence of
Arabia, although Mundy claimed otherwise. "In real
life Grim was an American officer attached to the British Intelligence in Palestine, where I met him in 1920.
He very kindly introduced me to the lewder fellows of

the baser sort with whom it was his business to deal. They were excellent company, as he was also, although he was a difficult man to understand."

Adventure's Writers' Brigade was too large to be discussed very thoroughly here. Among its other members were Georges Surdez, who lived in Brooklyn and specialized in tales of the Foreign Legion; Arthur O. Friel, who wrote serials about finding lost tribes in the South American jungles and had actually done that himself in 1922; H. Bedford-Jones, a prolific transplanted Canadian, who produced millions of words and was familiar with every period of history, every war and every minor skirmish—if there was any time in history when more than two people had gotten into a fight, H. Bedford-Jones could make a story out of it and tell you the exact weapons used. And there were authors whose very names hinted at adventure and exotic places—Rafael Sabatini, F. St. Mars, T. Samson Miller, Negley Farson, Raymond S. Spears, Romaine H. Lowdermilk. Not to mention such men of rank as Major Calvin B. Carter, Colonel George Brydges Rodney, Capt. George Warburton Lewis, Major George Fielding Eliot, General Rafael de Nogales and Major Malcolm Wheeler-Nicholson.

Major Nicholson, an ex-Cavalry officer, is the man who played an important part in killing off the pulp magazines. In 1934 the Major, after writing many pulp novelets about army action and an occasional historic yarn about the Borgias, decided to start his own comic book company. No one had as yet made a go of original, not newspaper reprint, comic books. Major Nicholson worked up a format combining pulp plots and action with funny paper directness. He hired out-of-work old-timers and young art students, paid little, and got out a line of magazines. One of his titles, not surprisingly, was *Adventure Comics*. The Major himself went broke and so it was his creditors who carried on with his line and its new titles

Action and *Detective.* These are the comic books that introduced Superman and Batman and drew huge audiences away from the pulp magazine.

Arthur S. Hoffman was hired away from *Adventure* in 1927. He spent a year editing a higher class magazine and then retired to Carmel, New York, where there is a lake. Several editors carried on at the magazine. In the middle '30's Popular Publications bought the title and Howard Bloomfield took over for a long stay as editor. The quality of *Adventure* held up for most of its pulp years, then began to slip in the late '40's. As did its nearest competitor *Short Stories.* First an expensive-paper magazine, *Short Stories* turned pulp in 1910. That was the year Doubleday acquired it and converted to an adventure pulp policy. Harry E. Maule, an ex-newspaper man, served as editor for most of the magazine's first twenty years as a pulp. *Short Stories* looked and acted like *Adventure*, right down to the little dingbats stuck in the text as illustrations. The readers here joined the Ends-of-the-Earth Club (with headquarters in Garden City, New York), sent their letters to the "Mail Bag" and instead of sitting round the Camp-Fire they gathered in the Story Teller's Circle.

Street & Smith packaged similar material in several magazines. *The Popular Magazine*, started as a juvenile, had gradually grown up. It published the work of Rex Beach, Jack London, John Buchan and Elmer Davis. In the early 1920's Street & Smith introduced *Complete Story*, an adventure pulp with no cliffhangers. This was actually an older pulpwood, *People's*, with a new name. *People's* dates back to 1906 and had become a fat 224-page magazine in its good years during the World War I period. *People's* featured not only stories of adventure and sports but even an occasional story about the business world. And *People's* ran more mystery stories. It was in this magazine that Frank L. Packard's Jimmie Dale stories first appeared. The work of this Canadian author is found mostly on thrift shop book shelves nowadays, but in the second and third decades of this century he had considerable renown. Jimmie Dale came out in books and in silent movies. Inspired probably by such earlier cracksmen as Raffles and O. Henry's Jimmy Valentine, Jimmie Dale did them one better. He had an alternate identity, that of the Grey Seal. He skulked through the midnight streets of New York, masked and mysterious. Hunted by the police, but actually a man dedicated to justice, he struck swiftly and left behind only a small sticker, the notorious grey seal. In the everyday world Jimmie Dale was a wealthy playboy and when he wasn't the Grey Seal he had several other identities to wear. In the next chapter you will see that the editors at Street & Smith were still thinking fondly of Jimmie Dale twenty years later.

Blue Book was a magazine that got going when there was also a *Green Book* and a *Red Book.* None of them were anything like Victorian England's *Yellow Book.* Whereas *Adventure* had been published by a ladies' dress pattern company, *Blue Book* owed its financing to ladies' hats. Louis Eckstein, founder of the Consolidated Magazines Corporation, had made his fortune in the millinery trade. *Blue Book* had begun as *The Monthly Story Magazine* in 1905 and changed its name in 1907. In the pre-World War I period it was a very sedate pulp and included a slick paper section of photos of stage personalities. It might carry a profile portrait of a pretty girl on the cover and for every adventure story there was likely to be a polite romantic one with a title like "Little Miss Cinderella." Like the Munsey pulps it was competing with, the early *Blue Book* was sparsely illustrated. Some stories were presented with only their titles hand-lettered and the most anybody got was a two- or three-inch high decorative title incorporating a simple line drawing. All this was to change.

In the 1920's, when *Blue Book* had become unabashedly

an adventure magazine, it was one of the most handsomely illustrated of the pulps. In the next decade there was no pulpwood fiction magazine that came near *Blue Book*. Through the '30's some of the major illustrators in America worked at illustrating what the magazine called its stirring short stories, remarkable serials and lively novelets. The *Blue Book* fiction of the 1930's was similar to that of *Adventure*, *Argosy* and *Short Stories*, though possibly a bit slicker. H. Bedford-Jones, Georges Surdez, Max Brand, W.C. Tuttle, Achmed Abdullah and similar action-fiction men appeared in its pages. So did Edgar Rice Burroughs and Tarzan. In terms of fiction, the magazine had several equals. No one came near it in terms of illustration. The reason was its editor, Donald Kennicott, who was in charge of the magazine from the '20's to its final sad days in the '50's. In Walt Reed's book *The Illustrator In America*, which covers all the magazine illustration of this century, the only samples of pulp work, with one exception, are from *Blue Book*. Kennicott, who acted as both story editor and art editor, paid no more for illustrations than most pulp editors and yet he got all sorts of artists to work for him. Every artist I've questioned gave me some variation of painter John Clymer's reasons for working for *Blue Book*. "Don Kennicott left me a very free hand as to choice of subject matter and the manner in which I handled the story and that was the reason it was so much fun to work for him." Of course in the Depression years making a living was the important thing for most young illustrators. Kennicott had the advantage by offering, besides a regular small income, encouragement and the chance to have fun.

One of the major artists to draw for Kennicott and *Blue Book* was Austin Briggs. When I talked to Briggs, at his Connecticut estate (which is several miles inland from the Westport-based Famous Artists School he lends his name to), he told me, "I'm one of the highest-paid artists of my period. Because of the chance I got with *Blue Book*. That, and fighting for money." Briggs had already worked very briefly in the slick-paper magazines in the late 1920's, when he was still in his teens. The Depression set in and he wasn't able to get enough work in the high paying markets. So he took some samples around to Kennicott. Kennicott liked his work and Briggs did pictures for the magazine throughout the '30's. He experimented with a number of techniques and got no interference. "Kennicott seemed to worry only about whether the hands and feet looked okay," Briggs recalls. His style in the early '30's was sketchy and based considerably on that of Joseph Coll, whose pen and ink drawings in *Collier's* and *Everybody's* in the first two decades of this century awed and inspired a good many growing artists. Briggs moved away from this style. He even did some *Blue Book* illustrations in grease pencil on window shade cloth. Since Kennicott was paying only $100 maximum for the four or five drawings each story required, Briggs took on other jobs. One of these was working on the pulp-like adventures of Flash Gordon. He was first assistant to Alex Raymond and then, when Raymond entered the service, he drew the page himself. Always thinking of getting back into the slicks, he never signed his name to the Flash Gordon strip. "I was ashamed of it," he says now. He left both Flash and Kennicott in the '40's and moved into the pages of *The Saturday Evening Post*. They hired him there because they'd been noticing his work in *Blue Book*.

Many other very good illustrators did pictures for *Blue Book*. The gaudy John Richard Flanagan; John Clymer, who specialized in historical pageantry; Frederick Chapman, whose work was precise and stark. The artist who did more illustrating in *Blue Book* than anyone else was a man with the unlikely name of Herbert Morton Stoops. From the mid-1930's on, Stoops painted almost every *Blue Book* cover and, using the more adventuresome penname of Jeremy Cannon, did hundreds of black and white interior illustrations. Stoops was a brilliant depictor of action and had an exceptional sense of light and shadow. He handled every period of history and every kind of battle and confrontation. He died in the late 1940's and by that time *Blue Book* was already in its decline. There is still a magazine called *Blue Book* today. Like the still surviving *Adventure*, it is an un-handsome non-fiction enterprise.

CHAPTER FOUR

A. K. A. THE SHADOW

The Shadow! This name puzzled him. He had heard talk of a Shadow—but no one had seemed to know who the man might be. The name was scarcely more than a myth among gangsters. Only a few had spoken of it; and they had said very little.

There were those, of course, who claimed that they had heard his voice coming through the spaceless ether over the radio. But at the broadcasting studios, The Shadow's identity had been carefully guarded. . . . Every Thursday night the spy from crookdom would contrive to be in the twisting corridor—watching the door of the room that was supposed to be The Shadow's. Yet no one ever entered that room!

Could it be, then, that The Shadow broadcast by remote control—that his voice was conveyed to the studio by private wire? No one knew. He and his fear-striking laugh had been heard—that was all.

—Maxwell Grant,
The Living Shadow

THEY wanted somebody to read detective stories over the radio. This was in the late 1920's and it didn't take much to make a radio show then. "Street & Smith's Detective Story Magazine Hour," put together by the Ruthrauff & Ryan advertising agency of New York, consisted of a man reading from the week's issue of the pulp magazine. You can always find an out-of-work actor in New York City, but still there was the problem of what exactly to call him. Simply to refer to him as "the man who reads the detective stories" isn't very chilling. The first actor Ruthrauff & Ryan used was named James La Curton. Perhaps it was the lack of mystery in his name which led one of the advertising agency's young writers to suggest calling their narrator The Shadow. Gradually the program went in for more production, stories were dramatized and The Shadow took to talking in a hollow voice and asking his listeners, "Who knows what evil lurks in the hearts of men?" Soon the Shadow was a modest celebrity in his own right and Street & Smith found that, almost by accident, they had a new and popular character. Being Street & Smith, they decided to make more money from him. To help on the project they hired an amateur magician from Philadelphia.

The young man was Walter B. Gibson, friend of, and ghost writer for, such magicians as Houdini, Blackstone and Thurston. Gibson was working as a staff writer for the Philadelphia Ledger Syndicate and had written some for true crime magazines and for a fleeting Bernarr MacFadden magazine named *True Strange*. Gibson says now he had not read much in the pulp field when he was asked to expand The Shadow from a radio voice into a pulp novel hero. He had read the book-length adventures of Street & Smith's earlier mysteryman Jimmie Dale and most of the major detective story writers of the time. "I was particularly fond of Arsene Lupin," Gibson told me. Lupin, the French super-thief created in 1907 by Maurice

Leblanc, specialized in intricate and audacious schemes and impenetrable disguises.

The editor Gibson first worked with was Frank Blackwell, whom he'd come in contact with while trying to crack the *Detective Story* market. Street & Smith were cautious with their new pulp and planned *The Shadow* magazine originally as a quarterly, telling Gibson if the number one issue went over they'd hire him to write three more. There wasn't much in the way of an art budget and when Gibson delivered his initial Shadow novel, "The Living Shadow," he was shown the left-over oil painting which had been dug out of the art department files to serve as the first cover of *The Shadow* magazine. It was the only piece of art anyone could find with a shadow on it. Unfortunately for Gibson the long dark shadow fell across the figure of a frightened Chinese. Having no Chinese characters in his story, Gibson had to return to Philadelphia and write one in. Gibson was given a new name by Street & Smith, too. He was to write the Shadow series as Maxwell Grant. *The Shadow* magazine was an immediate success. It soon changed from quarterly to monthly and then to twice a month publication. By the end of 1936 Gibson, who thought he'd be lucky to get to do the four novels he and Blackwell had contemplated, had written 112 book-length Shadow stories. When The Shadow concluded his magazine career in the summer of 1949 Gibson had produced roughly 280 novels about the character. He thinks he may have written more novels about a single character than any author ever.

The Shadow was not an easy man to get to know. In the first novels, in fact, even Gibson doesn't seem quite sure who he is. Unlike the Jimmie Dale novels, there are no interludes in the Maxwell Grant epics showing the real Shadow relaxing with friends before slipping into a disguise. The Shadow never appears before the reader undisguised. Often he lurks in the background, more like the sinister villain figure of a movie serial. He has a love of obfuscation and dim lighting and comes across as the kind of man who would wear a mask even when he's alone in a pitch black room. The early episodes concentrate on vanishings, fireworks, surprises and mysterious atmosphere with The Shadow himself almost too much of a phantom. The effect is something like a magic show with lots of tricks and no star magician. The Shadow novels are, especially those of the early '30's, usually about the people he works on and through, the crooks he destroys and the agents he manipulates. Gradually The Shadow acquired an assortment of alter egos. His best known pseudo-identity was Lamont Cranston, millionaire playboy. He also took to appearing as Fritz, the janitor at police headquarters. Eventually, in the late 1930's, it was made known that The Shadow was actually a noted aviator named Kent Allard. By this time most people thought he was actually Lamont Cranston. Even some of the writers who filled in as Maxwell Grant after Gibson seem to have believed this and written accordingly.

Always, like any good executive, able to delegate work, The Shadow used a large and diversified staff. "He works as a lone hand," explained a blurb, "yet he has able aides in Harry Vincent, a presentable young man who can make himself at home anywhere; Burbank, who serves as communications contact for all the agents; Clyde Burke, reporter on the *Classic*; Cliff Marsland, who served a term in prison for a crime he did not commit and whose innocence was known only to The Shadow. Marsland, rather than show that innocence, was willing to work for The Shadow as a branded crook, for The Shadow had rescued him from death in the past. Mann, the calm-looking broker, is another link in The Shadow's small but compact army of crime-busters." He also frequently relied on a cab driver named Moe Shrevnitz. The professional end of crime-busting is represented by Commissioner Weston, like Lamont Cranston a member of New York's exclusive Cobalt Club, and Joe Cardona, ace detective of New York headquarters. "Cardona was acknowledged as a leader in his profession . . . His dark eyes were keen; his firm jaw marked him as a man of action."

Walter Gibson is proud of the hundreds of gimmicks, intrigues and villainies he invented during his long tenure with The Shadow, and of the wide range of localities he used for dark deeds and swift retribution. One of Gibson's specialties was the evocative opening, and he told me that in the cases where his novels turned out too short he'd usually lengthen them by adding to the starting scene. He didn't think much of the pulp novelists who, like his friend Lester Dent, started off with a bang. Gibson preferred:

> Long Island Sound lay blanketed with a dense, sullen mist. From the shore, the heavy fog appeared as a grimy mass of solid blackness. The scene was one of swirling, impenetrable night, for not a gleam of light disturbed the omnipresent darkness.
>
> No eye could have discerned the spot where the shore ceased and water began. The rocks beside the beach were invisible, and so was the man who stood near them. The only token of his presence was the sound of his slow, steady breathing, broken by the low, impatient growls that came muffled from his throat.

And:

> Bulky, blackish in the thick night fog, the steamship *Ozark* loomed beside her North River pier, where busy stevedores were loading the last items of the freighter's cargo.
>
> Feeble pier lights were kindly to the *Ozark*. Dimmed by

the fog, their glow did not reveal the scratched, unpainted portions of the steamer's sides.

Gibson saved the high gear prose for later in the story, especially for the fearful confrontations between the avenging Shadow and the current representatives of crookdom.

Streaming bullets battered the wall beyond The Shadow. A gun resting on the inner edge of the depressed opening, The Shadow jabbed shots from the level of the garage floor.

There was a furious cry from Pointer Trame. Behind the boxes, he had seen what happened. He spotted the outline of the pit and saw his chance to attack the lone fighter who had chosen it as a fort. Along the wall came Pointer, lunging for the hole.

He was above it, driving his gun downward. This time the revolver held real bullets. He thought he saw The Shadow in that lower blackness. Pointer tugged the trigger, delivering a rapid fire. His bullets spattered the slime.

From another corner of the pit, the spurt of a gun flashed upward, knifing a bullet into the body of Pointer Trame. The big-shot wavered, gripping his side. Just then, the machine gun resumed a last spasmodic burst.

Its muzzle faced the big-shot. His sagging form was flayed by a metal hail. Swept from his feet, the bullet-riddled body of Trame tumbled into the pit beside The Shadow, dead before he struck.

Sidestepping that shattered corpse, The Shadow again aimed for the machine gun. No shots were needed. Vic Marquette and his reserves had ended the brief outburst.

Placing his automatic beneath his cloak, The Shadow strode to the darkness at the rear of the garage and merged with the night beyond.

Oftentimes the Shadow was quite exultant during showdowns:

Then, with a spinning side twist, he cleared the counter of the shooting gallery, whirled about and opened fire with a pair of automatics. The men with the rifles dropped back, firing wildly, in this most singular of scenes. The Shadow was jabbing shots from the darkness below the targets and it looked as though the shooting gallery had begun to back-fire on its customers. Rifle shots, aimed high, were knocking ducks from racks and ringing metal bells, but none found The Shadow. His laugh, rising above the discordant chorus, invited wilder fire.

And:

All three turned toward the spot from which the sound had come. They were staring directly at the torture casket in which Harry Vincent had once been.

Now a black form emerged from the opening in the top. The astounded counterfeiters were staring into the muzzles of two revolvers—held by The Shadow!

A taunting, uncanny laugh came from the figure in black. Its mirthless tones quivered from the walls of the eerie cavern. It seemed to be the laugh of doom.

"So the three of you came back," mocked the weird whispered voice of The Shadow. "I expected you. Now you are here—to answer for your crimes."

Walter Gibson stuck with the Shadow until the middle of 1946, then quit after a disagreement with the new administration at Street & Smith. At this point he had written approximately 270 novels about his character. These included "The Shadow Laughs," "The Red Menace," "The Ghost Makers," "The Black Hush," "The Blue Sphinx," "The London Crimes," "Death Rides The Skyway," "The Gray Ghost," "The Crystal Buddha," "The Green Hoods," "The Invincible Shiwan Khan," "The Wasp Returns," "The Robot Master," "The White Skulls" and "Mother Goose Murders." From 1936 on, Gibson shared the Maxwell Grant penname with Theodore Tinsley. Tinsley, whose brother was the aviation illustrator Frank Tinsley, was a frequent contributor to the pulp magazines during the decade of the '30's. He did a series about a tough Broadway columnist for *Black Mask* and wrote of a hardboiled lady detective named Carrie Cashin for Street & Smith's short-lived *Crime Busters* magazine. Tinsley's first Shadow novel appeared in the November 1, 1936, issue and he did four a year from then until August, 1943 when the magazine went back to being a monthly. There is one other novel from this period that Gibson doesn't take full credit for. A Miami-based story titled "The Golden Vulture," it is a rewrite of a novel written by Lester Dent. Just why Dent, the chief author of the Doc Savage novels, turned out a Shadow story, Gibson no longer recalls. During Gibson's estrangement from Street & Smith, Bruce Elliott, who was also an amateur magician, did about a dozen or more of the Shadow novels. These stories, with titles like "Murder On Main St." and "Jabberwocky Thrust," abandoned much of the format and trappings of the series and used Lamont Cranston as an amateur private investigator. They are considerably less melodramatic than the usual Shadow novel and seem clearly an attempt to update the character. Apparently this did not work and in 1948 Gibson was invited to come back and be Maxwell Grant once more. He only got to do five new Shadow novels and then the magazine abruptly folded. This surprised Gibson and his editor as well. By this time, early in 1949, *The Shadow* had dropped to quarterly publication and was being edited by Daisy Bacon, who had made *Love Story* the best selling romance pulp in the country. "Before I could really get to work on them," Daisy Bacon told me, "Street & Smith suddenly discontinued the fiction line. These two magazines had had pretty brutal handling but with patience and careful tending, I believe a great deal could have been done with them." The other magazine she refers to was *Doc Savage*.

Though the slouch-hatted and cloaked Shadow is, even now, a familiar figure, for awhile in the early 1930s no one at Street & Smith could decide what he looked like. After a spell of not appearing on the cover of the magazine at all, he started showing up in a cloak and hood, looking something like a black monk. Inside the magazine he appeared on the contents page with a skeletal face and wearing a fedora. Gradually the sharp nosed, slouch-hatted Shadow evolved. The early Shadow covers were by Jerome Rozen and legend has it that an early model for the shadowy avenger was associate art editor Bill Lawlor. He is said to have kept a cape and wide-brimmed hat hanging in a corner of his office. An early illustrator of the Shadow novels was Tom Lovell. Now a well-known commercial artist, Lovell worked on The Shadow in the early '30's when he was fresh out of Syracuse University with a Bachelor of Fine Arts degree. Lovell explained his working methods to me this way: "My wife, who also posed for all the imperiled girls, would read all the manuscripts and mark action spots for me, incidently picking up a very un-ladylike vocabulary of gangster slang . . . I 'faked' everything in the interior illustrations. That is, I drew from the mirror or my head, which was great training . . . I did a dozen or so illustrations for The Shadow each month at $12 per."

After Lovell, the interior work on The Shadow was done by Ed Cartier and Earl Mayan. Cartier, who is probably best remembered for his work in the science fiction field, attended New York's Pratt Institute, as did Mayan, later a frequent *Saturday Evening Post* illustrator. In the late 1930's the two men shared a studio, which accounts for the similarity of their work. "During the two years after school and before the 2nd World War Ed and I roomed together in a brownstone up on East 72nd Street," Mayan recalls. "Street & Smith paid highly for our services, compared to some of the others. $12.50 for a single and twenty-five dollars for a double spread. I did The Shadow on a regular basis after Tom Lovell moved up the ladder of success . . . Ed and I remained together in this brownstone sharing expenses and windows. We each worked at one of the two windows in the flat, where, even so, the light was very dim . . . We were succeeding as illustrators, but our success (in barely meeting the rent) was interrupted by the war." As to how they worked, Mayan explained to me, "In a novel length job like The Shadow you had to space your scenes. . . . The necessary thing at all times was action. You'd get eaten out if you didn't provide this. With the title page illustrations, content didn't matter so long as it had action, mood, horror, something to stir the reader."

During the war years, much of The Shadow illustration was handled by Paul Orban, a Street & Smith regular since the early days of the Depression. When Orban drew Shadow pictures the price had risen to fifteen dollars. After the war S.R. Powell, a comic book artist with a thick-lined chunky style, took on the job of illuminating the Maxwell Grant manuscripts. Ed Cartier then returned for what turned out to be his last fling as an illustrator. The final Shadow stories were illustrated by reliable Paul Orban with covers by Rozen, the man who'd started it all off back in 1931.

Unlike the majority of pulp mystery men, The Shadow enjoyed a moderate success in other media. After going from radio to pulps, the character went back onto radio. The new radio show was based on the magazine format, though simplified. The Shadow had only one alternate self now, that of Lamont Cranston. He acquired a female companion, Margot Lane, and the ability to cloud men's minds and be invisible. The pulp novels borrowed Margot but never the invisibility knack. Walter Gibson recalls woodshedding up in Maine with a then prominent radio crime writer named Edward Hale Bierstadt. They worked on a script for the show. A series of disagreements developed, involving Gibson and the advertising agency producing the show, and nothing from the Gibson-Bierstadt collaboration reached the air. Then the program finally appeared, sponsored in the East by Blue Coal. Robert Hardy Andrews played the role of The Shadow. Andrews, a writer who lays claim to having invented the soap opera, was followed by Orson Welles. This was prior to his Martian invasion broadcast and the young Welles was earning extra money by moonlighting from his Mercury Theatre of the Air. Agnes Moorehead played Margot Lane and the two must have been one of the more interesting romantic teams in radio. By the 1940's Bret Morrison had settled into the part of Lamont Cranston.

Meanwhile The Shadow was also having a low budget movie career. The first screen Shadow was silent film leftover Rod La Rocque. After him came Victor Jory and finally the pride of Hollywood's poverty row, Kane Richmond. Although he wasn't a box office smash, The Shadow did better in the movies than he did in the newspapers. Walter Gibson wrote the continuity for a transient comic strip which his old employers, the Ledger Syndicate, distributed prior to World War II. The cartoonist on the feature was Vernon Greene, whose previous credit was the unlikely one of ghosting the pretty-girl strip, *Polly & Her Pals*. The Shadow strip didn't succeed but Gibson and Greene salvaged the original drawings, cut them in pieces and turned them into comic book pages. The Shadow comic book followed, early in 1940. This was the only comic book with oil paintings for covers, since the always economical Street & Smith were using old Shadow pulp art. The first issue of the comic book served as a testing ground for several other properties. Besides the Shadow lead off, there were strips devoted to Doc

Savage, Nick Carter, Frank Merriwell and a cartoon adaptation of a Horatio Alger, Jr. story. Street & Smith, taking no chances, tried everything that had appealed to boys in the whole ninety years of their existence. There was also an ad for the Shadow Official Holster Set, with gun, mask, handcuffs, whistle and flashlight.

While The Shadow had been waxing and proliferating, Street & Smith had been cautiously planning how best to repeat their achievement. Two years after the debut of The Shadow they were ready to launch some new single character pulps. In 1933 came Doc Savage, to be considered in a later chapter, and Nick Carter. "In February W.H. Ralston had John Nanovice bring me into his august presence," recalls Richard Wormser. "The Shadow had been so successful that they were going to revive Nick Carter, who had been off the stands since about 1924. Could I write a novel every other week? Being young, ignorant and hungry I said sure and became Nick Carter." *Nick Carter Magazine* came out in the spring of 1933, a 10¢ monthly that featured a Nick Carter novel and a Nick Carter short story. Wormser wrote the novels under the penname Nick Carter. There was in the magazine, as in most Street & Smith pulps aimed primarily at juveniles, a club to join for a dime. This was called simply the Nick Carter Club and for your ten cents you got a Nick Carter badge. For another ten cents you could get a rubber stamp. For free you got advice and crime lore in the club section of the magazine. For instance, the June, 1934, issue passes on "the advice Nick Carter received from his illustrious father, and according to which he has patterned his life." The senior Carter's words to live by were, "Keep your body, your clothing, and your conscience clean."

Richard Wormser had a pretty strict code to write by, too. "Nick Carter had tough sledding. We couldn't use anything suggestive of The Shadow. . . . No character could have a discernible ethnic background, crooks couldn't shoot back at policemen, criminals couldn't use cars because the auto industry might resent it." Originally planned as a twice a month publication, Nick Carter's magazine stayed monthly. "So I didn't write a novel every other week," says Wormser. "I wrote seventeen in ten months, however, and received a little less than five thousand dollars for a little more than a million words. That was good money for that lowest of 20th century years. . . . After seventeen issues, Nick was closed down again."

The 1930's pulp Nick Carter was not exactly like the earlier Nick Carter. In a study of the entire career of the master detective, E.S. Turner had these observations about Nick's pulp incarnation:

> Carter was by now very busy and very rich; too busy to observe the normal courtesies, and perhaps too rich to care. He lived in a house on Fifth Avenue with a Filipino valet "whose name was changed every time Nick Carter felt like it." Nick was now tackling big gangster organizations and kidnappers. . . . One out-of-the-way case involved the recovery of a stolen yacht loaded with a drug which had been hailed as the new anaesthetic, but which, belatedly, had been found to drive patients crazy and give them the characteristics of apes. Carter searched for the yacht from his airplane, which was fitted with a large magnifying glass in the floor. Being Nick Carter, he was allowed to mount offensive weapons on his aircraft and to carry bombs, even while flying over New York.
>
> Certainly Nick Carter set an example of incorruptibility. To a father who offered him two million dollars to save his son from the consequences of his folly, he merely said, "Your son is going to burn."
>
> He had become a very hard man indeed.

In their other major tries at duplicating the sales triumphs of The Shadow, Street & Smith continued to stay close to what had already worked. The Whisperer, initiated in 1936, was a near duplicate of the Shadow. "A low, mirthless chuckle, an awesome whisper of defiance, as a half visible wraith moves through the night," is how the standard blurb described him. "Criminals flee at this eerie challenge, for it announces the arrival of the mysterious nemesis of crime, for whom there are no rules or regulations deterrent in the path of justice." The Whisperer's vigilante aspect is heightened further by the fact he's a policeman by day. James "Wildcat" Gordon, New York's youngest police commissioner, "known for his hard-hitting, unorthodox methods for solving crime. As The Whisperer, there are no rules, no interfering politicians to decree how a case is to be solved and slow the swift path of justice." The Whisperer, also known as The Long Arm of Justice, had his own magazine and was an occasional performer in other Street & Smith pulps. Attributed to Clifford Goodrich, the Whisperer stories were the work of Norman Daniels and Alan Hathway. Hathway, later the managing editor of *Newsday*, took over the character in 1940 and stayed with it until its termination in 1942.

Another notable contender, The Avenger, was introduced in the late 1930's, built out of scraps of The Shadow and Doc Savage. To give him an extra nudge toward success Street & Smith signed the name Kenneth Robeson to The Avenger novels and billed them as by The Famous Creator of Doc Savage. Actually they were the work of a writer named Paul Ernst. Though Walter Gibson recalls that he and Lester Dent, the original Kenneth Robeson, did sit in on several of the conferences that resulted in the new character. Reversing the usual process, The Avenger got younger and better looking as time passed. In 1939 he has "a white, awesome, moveless face . . . colorless eyes, flaming like ice under a polar dawn." Plus which "The Avenger had no store of small talk. Quiet, invariably polite, he was yet as blunt and direct as a machine." By 1942 the reader is told "The Avenger was young. Very young. He was in his twenties, though his habit of command, his level, dominating voice and vibrant power of personality, gave him the impact of a man much older." Through all the changes of person and personality, brought on probably by inadequate sales figures, The Avenger's approach to law and order remained the same. In his layman's identity he was Richard Henry Benson, "backed by a tremendous wealth accumulated in his early years of adventuring throughout the world and equipped with a profound knowledge of any field and practice." After his wife and child were killed by gangsters, Benson "founded the compact crime-fighting unit of Justice, Inc., dedicating his life to smashing the underworld so that innocent lives of others might not be seared as his had been." Like some of today's dedicated social avengers, Benson lived in Greenwich Village. The Avenger had quite a crew working under him at Justice, Inc. "There is the six-foot-nine, near three-hundred-pound giant, Algernon Heathcote Smith—better call him Smitty— whose vast strength is probably second only to his inventive genius in the electrical-engineering field. Then there is the dour Scot, Fergus MacMurdie, the head of The Avenger's crime laboratory. Mac, himself, is one of the country's leading chemists. . . . And last we have the Negro couple, Joshua Elijah H. Newton and his attractive wife, Rosabel. No one would suspect from their role of languid servants that both are honor graduates of famed Tuskegee Institute and, like the others in Dick Benson's crew, strong in heart and mind in furthering their unending battle against crime." Josh Newton, though broadly done, is one of the few intelligent black men in the pulps. His Uncle Tom act puts down not only the stories' villains but the stock attitudes of many other pulp writers.

CHAPTER FIVE

THANK YOU, MASKED MAN

"David was eighteen when I saw him. . . . He seemed to be
hallucinated and acted in various somewhat odd ways. For
instance, he attended lectures in a cloak, which he wore
over his shoulders and arms; he carried a cane; his whole
manner was entirely artificial. . . . By always playing a part
he found he could in some measure overcome his shyness,
self-consciousness and vulnerability. He found reassur-
ance in the consideration that whatever he was doing he
was not being himself."

—R.D. Laing,
The Divided Self

"Hey, masked man, what the hell is your story? How come
you never wait for thank you's?"

—*Lenny Bruce*

PULP publishers kept busy in the early years of the
Depression jumping on bandwagons. One of the easiest
successes to emulate was that of Street & Smith's Shadow.

You could set up as a mystery man almost as simply as a kid could play at it. All you needed was a cape, a mask and an awesome name. Walter Gibson's contemporaries had shared many of the entertainments of his growing up years and they, too, were able to blend old Jimmie Dale plots with memories of innumerable silent movie serials. They remembered also those stirring names that had flashed on the screen. The Spider, The Phantom, etc. Within two years of the advent of The Shadow, the mystery man pulp was a flourishing genre.

In the summer of 1933 Popular Publications broke into the mystery man business with *The Spider* magazine. Billed as "a new magazine with a dynamite punch," the ten-cent monthly featured a novel entitled "The Spider Strikes" in its maiden issue. In his first adventures The Spider behaves in the accepted Jimmie Dale manner, but instead of grey seals he leaves behind seals featuring "a reproduction, in blood-red, of a particularly hideous spider." In everyday life The Spider is Richard Wentworth, world traveler and New York clubman. "You'll love Richard Wentworth, once you meet him," promised ads in the Popular pulps. "And you'll love the one woman in all the world who shares his deadly secret—Nita Van Sloan." Figuring that was enough love, Popular went on to say, "You'll get to like his quiet Hindu servant, Ram Singh." Along with the unsuspecting Inspector Kirkpatrick, this was the running cast of the Spider epics.

The first two Spider novels were credited to R.T.M. Scott. Scott, whose triple initials stood for Reginald Thomas Maitland, was a Canadian-born author who migrated to the United States shortly after the first World War. Popular called him "one of the finest mystery-action writers of the present day," though they soon replaced him with somebody else. In his early forties when he launched the Spider, R.T.M. Scott was mainly known then for a series of books and stories about a character named Secret Service Smith. Scott, having worked in engineering in India, Australia and Italy and having served as an Infantry major in the war, was well stocked with story backgrounds. Characters were something else again and when it came time to produce a new novel series, he borrowed considerably from his Smith stories. Whereas Richard Wentworth is served by Ram Singh, Smith has a huge Hindu servant named Langa Doonh. Instead of Nita Van Sloan, Smith is aided by the remarkably pretty Bernice Asterly. Known to his intimates by the first name Aurelius, Smith does not actually work for the Secret Service anymore and functions for the most part as a consulting detective and freelance avenger. He had the same languid playboy manner that Wentworth later affected. One of Scott's mystery-action Secret Service Smith novels, for instance, begins: "It was toward the close of an afternoon in Spring that Aurelius Smith, behind his great, flat-topped table, leaned back in his chair and softly tinkled an antique temple bell." Readers and reviewers of the 1920's seemed to find Secret Service Smith admirable. One of Scott's few detractors in the '20's was the then obscure Dashiell Hammett. Writing in the *Saturday Review of Literature*, Hammett said the stories were "mechanical and preposterously motivated . . . Smith is one of the always popular deducers, though not a very subtle specimen." Among his many abilities Secret Service Smith included hypnotism and voice-throwing.

In The Spider pulp novels that Scott wrote in 1933 the Aurelius Smith mannerisms were carried on. One lovely touch in the first Spider adventure is Richard Wentworth's courting of Nita by transatlantic radio:

> Later that night, Wentworth, clad in black pajamas and propped up by pillows on his bed, held his muted violin to his chin and played low, throbbing music. Much of the music was improvised and seemed to express a longing for

something unobtainable in its mingled sadness and sweetness. Ram Singh squatted on the floor in the sitting room, his body slightly swaying with the rhythm of the music. Richard Wentworth could have been a great musician if he had taken up the violin professionally.

Abruptly the violinist placed his instrument by his side and took up the hand telephone from the little table by his bed.

"Ship to shore service," he requested and gave a New York City telephone number.

In a remarkably short time, such progress has science made, a feminine voice came across the expanse of ocean, a low, throaty voice, vibrant of life upon a spring day. For a few moments Wentworth spoke in French, the modern language of love, and in his voice was some of the longing of the music he had been playing.

Presently Ram Singh was summoned to the bedroom and, as he had done before on several occasions, held the telephone to his master's ear while the violin was again taken up. Softly Wentworth began to play Kreisler's *Caprice Viennois.*

Wentworth's performance, by the way, takes place just after he has shot and killed a man and fastened a Spider seal next to the bullet hole in the corpse's forehead.

The problems Scott gave The Spider to cope with were, by pulp standards, pretty prosaic. In "The Spider Strikes" Wentworth tangles with a master criminal who has a flair for impersonations and in "The Wheel of Death," the Spider, doing a few impersonations himself, puts a sinister gambling establishment out of business. Bigger and better struggles were in store for Richard Wentworth. Commencing with the December, 1933 issue a new name is signed to the Spider chronicles. It is one of the great fake-sounding pennames of the pulps—Grant Stockbridge. The name, with its echoes of Maxwell Grant and staid New England towns, seems to have been used most often by the prolific Norvell W. Page. Page often appeared in editorial offices wearing a cape himself and under his guidance The Spider graduated to more flamboyant, often cosmic, troubles. Even the titles of the monthly novels became more startling: "Wings Of The Black Death," "The Serpents Of Destruction," "Satan's Death Blast," "The Devil's Death Dwarfs," "The Claws Of The Gold Dragon," etc. The Spider deals, after his brief R.T.M. Scott phase, with "a city swept by Bubonic Plague," with an epidemic that turns America's finest families into a "set of swanky thieves and killers," with the Emperor of Hades, who "scattered his scarlet, slaying devil-dust" over New York, with 5,000 mad dogs who are rampaging in Cologne, Ohio and with dozens of other equally unsettling problems.

In the Stockbridge version Richard Wentworth takes to roaming Manhattan in a "ruthless and terrible" disguise. His nose "altered by putty, became hawk-like and predatory. His lips disappeared, so that his mouth was a gash. False, bushy brows, a lank, black wig. . . . A black jersey covered his formal shirt, a cape for his shoulders, a broad-brimmed black hat." All in all, a sinister version of a dirty old man. The Spider continued well into the '40's, though his popularity was at its peak a few years earlier. In the late 1930's, the Spider even appeared in the movies. As Popular Publications explained it, "Columbia Pictures Corporation has put the Spider on the silver-screen in a thrilling, heart-hammering, fifteen-part Chapter-play, *The Spider's Web.*" Warren Hull, later to become a television quizmaster, starred as Richard Wentworth.

Another early and successful competitor of The Shadow was The Phantom Detective. A product of the Thrilling pulp works, the *Phantom Detective* magazine got under way in February of 1933. The Phantom had become a detective out of boredom, a common complaint among rich playboys. "Born of wealthy parents who died

when he was a child, Richard Curtis Van Loan had grown
up under the competent tutelage of Frank Havens, millionaire newspaper publisher," explained an early novel.
"But Van felt stifled by the smugness of the people around
him and the sort of lives they led. He tried big-game hunting, deep-sea fishing, polo, other sports. All these eventually lost their appeal. He was bored—desperately, terribly
bored." Service in World War I had cheered Van up, but
then came the Armistice and the same old Park Avenue
boredom again. "It was during one of these periods that
Van, at Frank Havens' suggestion, tried his hand at solving a minor crime that stumped the police. He was successful—startlingly so. And he found his true vocation at
last. Hunting criminals, matching wits with them, supplied the element of danger and excitement that he
craved. Richard Curtis Van Loan became The Phantom."

Van followed his vocation for more than twenty years
and the *Phantom Detective* pulp did not cease publication until the middle of 1953. By that time The Phantom,
wearing either top hat and mask or one of his many disguises, had worked on well over a hundred and fifty
crimes. These included the problems of "The Race
Horses of Death," "The Listening Eyes," "The Movie Lot
Murders," "The Daggers of Kali," "The Tick-Tack-Toe
Murders" and "The Crime of Fu Kee Wong." The Phantom also provided employment for a large assortment of
writers. The first year of Phantom stories was credited to
G. Wayman Jones and the dozens thereafter to Robert
Wallace. Leo Margulies, the editorial director of all the
Thrilling pulp magazines, doesn't remember how he
made up the Jones penname. But Robert Wallace came
about because "Edgar Wallace was very big at the time."
One of the earliest writers of the Phantom Detective mysteries, and possibly the creator of the series, was D.L.
Champion. Champion's first name was D'Arcy and,
though he didn't get much opportunity to exercise them

with The Phantom Detective, his writing specialties were true crime and humor. Many of his most ingenious plots were used not in his stories but in getting quick money out of Margulies. After he noticed that the Thrilling editorial director only glanced at the first few and last few pages of a novel manuscript before issuing a pay voucher, Champion took to writing only those pages. He'd turn those in, sandwiched around blank paper, pay off his most urgent bills and wait for Margulies to call up and demand the rest of the Phantom. By 1940 Champion had graduated to *Black Mask* and his own byline. Among the many other writers who ghosted The Phantom Detective were Robert Sidney Bowen, Anatole France Feldman, Norman Daniels and W.T. Ballard.

Yet another of the Thrilling bunch of trick suit avengers was the Black Bat. The Bat was an impatient representative of law and order who went in for vigilante short cuts. In real life, or at least what passed for real life in the *Black Book Detective* novels featuring him, the Black Bat is Assistant District Attorney Tony Quinn. Once Quinn had been blinded by "certain desperate crooks in a mad effort to destroy evidence." The world still believes Quinn blind but, thanks to a secret eye transplant, "not only can he see perfectly, but—he can see in the blackest darkness. To him, even pastel shades are visible in a jet black room." As a DA, Quinn "fought crime and criminals with the relentlessness of the full majesty of the law—which can groan and creak at times." And so Quinn felt compelled to hurry things along as the Black Bat, "a man who prowled the night as noiselessly as a wraith, and whose name brought respect and fear from the most hardened criminal, and a man to whom many of the police who admired him—but not all—were grateful. The Black Bat fought criminals with their own methods. Ruthless, with a disregard for the law, he made his own rules as he went along. Here was a man who could fight with fists, or guns or knives . . ." Here is an example of the Bat confronting a crook on his own terms:

> The Black Bat stepped behind a tree. Peering through the darkness he located the man who stalked him. Carefully now, the Black Bat moved to cut this man off . . . the Black Bat could see in darkness while his opponent had to stumble around. As the man passed by, the Black Bat leaped out, wound an arm around his throat and muffled any cry. . . . Then he held him at arm's length, studied the young face, now mottled from being choked, and sent home a haymaker.

The Black Bat prose is credited to G. Wayman Jones, the house name again masking anybody who needed a fast penny a word. Though the novels didn't describe him as such, the Bat showed up on the covers and in the illustrations as a very close relative of Batman.

Next to Thrilling, Leo Margulies liked the word Masked best. He would put it in front of generic names and get new pulps. Magazines such as *Masked Detective* and *Masked Rider Western.* The Masked Rider began his career in the late 1930's. There was no continuing penname and all sorts of authors, real and imaginary, got credit: Tom Curry, Donald Bayne Hobart, Oscar J. Friend, etc. Often referred to as the Robin Hood outlaw, the Masked Rider was in reality Wayne Morgan. He rode a stallion called Midnight and had for a partner a Yaqui Indian named Blue Hawk. The Masked Detective started up a year or so later than the Rider. The detective novels were credited to C.K.M. Scanlon and could have been written by anybody. C.K.M. are the initials of Leo Margulies' wife and Scanlon was somebody who worked in the office. The penname was stuck on a number of writers. "I can't recall all the names I used," Norman Daniels told me. "A few, such as G. Wayman Jones, Dan Fowler,

C.K.M. Scanlon, Norman Judd, Kerry McRoberts come to mind, but mostly they've slipped my memory." Whoever the Masked Detective Scanlon was, he must have listened to the radio. As the Masked Rider authors were inspired by the Lone Ranger, he was stimulated by the Green Hornet radio show. The Masked Detective was actually Rex Parker, ace crime reporter on the *New York Comet* and so handsome "he might have been mistaken for a movie star." Only two people in the world knew of his dual identity and apparently not many more cared. The magazine folded early on.

The Ghost, too, had a relatively short career. He was featured in the Thrilling pulp of the same name, which commenced in January, 1940. In his initial case the Ghost "tackles the puzzling problem of the lisping man murders." As a slight switch on the usual presentation, the Ghost stories are told in the first person by George Chance, magician and detective, who is the Ghost himself. To add to the verisimilitude George Chance is listed as the author of the novels, too. The Ghost had an unusual background and set of capabilities. "I was born in the show business," he told his readers. "My father was an animal trainer and my mother a trapeze performer in the circus. . . . Thanks to early circus training, I am a fair tumbler and contortionist. I learned much of the secrets of makeup from a clown named Ricki. To the grave-eyed man who traveled with the show under the name of Don Avigne, I am indebted for knowledge that has made the knife one of the deadliest of weapons in my hands. Then there was Professor Gabby, who taught me principles of ventriloquism which are today responsible for the hundreds of voices of the Ghost. But most important of all, while I was hanging around the circus, I won the confidence of Marko, the magician. . . . I still have the billiard balls Marko gave me."

Chance worked as a detective with the knowledge and

approval of New York police commissioner Standish.
Commissioner Standish, like many pulp police men, had
a fondness for gimmickry and an impatience with legal
red tape. A tricky private avenger was something he believed New York needed. To help out in difficult police
cases handsome professional magician Chance turned
himself into the fearsome Ghost. "To create the character
of the Ghost, I take small wire ovals and put them into my
nose, tilting the tip and elongating the nostrils. For somewhat ghastly effect proper to a ghost-character, I darken
the inside of each nostril. Simple,eh—yet one must know
how. . . . Pallor comes out of a powderbox. I highlight my
naturally prominent cheek bones. Over my own teeth I
place shells the color of old ivory. After that, I have only
to affect a fixed vacuity of expression." The Ghost's circle
included a man who looked just like him, a glamour girl
named Merry White and a midget. After clearing up such
problems as "The Case of the Flaming Fist" and "The
Case of the Laughing Corpse," the Ghost did his final trick
and vanished from the newsstands. When asked who
wrote as George Chance, Leo Margulies replied, "I think
it was G.T. Fleming-Roberts."

Author G.T. Fleming-Roberts, who appears to have
been real despite his manufactured-sounding name,
worked on the sagas of several other phantom avengers.
In the early 1940's he wrote novels about the Black Hood
for a transitory pulp called *Hooded Detective*. The Black
Hood has the distinction of being a flop in both pulps and
comic books. In the comic book, *Top-Notch*, he got an only
slightly better grip on the public. In the Hood novels another impatient policeman becomes a masked detective.
It came about this way:

> Once he had been a member of New York's police force
> until he had been framed by a notorious criminal who
> called himself the Skull. Arrested for a crime he had not

committed, the young cop who was later to live under the alias Kip Burland, had jumped bail in an effort to hunt down the real criminal and clear himself. Once again he had crossed the trail of the Skull and this time the Skull's men had taken him out of the city, pumped six lead slugs into his body, and left him for dead. Except for the careful nursing of the Hermit, a whiskered old man who dwelled alone in a cabin in the Catskills, Kip Burland would not have lived.

The Hermit fills Kip with strength, health and chutzpah and Burland becomes the Black Hood, "merciless hunter of criminals." As usual the police frowned on him because they "did not understand the Black Hood's unorthodox methods." These misunderstood Hood methods include breaking and entering, kidnapping, extortion and assault with a deadly weapon.

Fleming-Roberts holds the distinction of having worked on the last of the pulp avengers. Late in 1949, when the pulp magazines were already diminishing, he wrote Captain Zero for Popular Publications. Zero, whose real name was Lee Allyn, turned invisible every night at midnight. This happened, an unfortunate side effect of some experiments at the famed Lockridge Research Foundation near Chicago, whether Allyn wanted to disappear or not. He'd considered his wild talent a liability until Steve Rice, reform-minded publisher of the *World*, had said to him, "I can use you, Allyn, in my clean-up campaign. You'll be my captain. Captain Zero. How's that for a name for nothingness?" Allyn worked as a reporter on the *World* and both he and his boss were impatient with the law's delays. Captain Zero, also known as the Master of Midnight, spent his short career eavesdropping and annoying suspects. While he was invisible he spoke in italics.

Back in the 1930's, when avengers blossomed, one of the

best known was the Moon Man. The creation of Frederick
C. Davis, Moon Man appeared quite regularly in *Ten Detective Aces*. By day Moon Man was Detective Sergeant
Steve Thatcher. Not only was he a policeman, but his
father was one as well. In fact, old Peter Thatcher was
Chief of Police, though unaware of his son's other identity. Chief Thatcher and the rest of the force thought of
Moon Man as nothing better than a "notorious criminal
who robbed the rich." Young Steve Thatcher had one of
the more striking mystery man getups. "Watching the
door, Thatcher quickly opened the small case he had carried in. From it he unrolled a long, voluminous black
robe. He drew it over his shoulders swiftly. On his hands
he pulled black gloves. He lifted carefully from the suit-
case a sphere of silver glass—the precious mask of the
Moon Man—and placed it over his head. Steve Thatcher
vanished and the Moon Man appeared." Recalling the
days of Moon Man and such adventures as "Crimson
Shackles," "Silver Death," and "Blood Barrier," Frederick C. Davis said recently, "I don't remember exactly
where the Moon Man idea came from except that at the
time Argus (one-way) glass was a novelty, and I was always looking for novelties. . . . I liked doing him and I kept
him going, a novelette every month, for about five years."

Quite a few pulp avengers sought to emulate Leslie
Charteris' Saint. In the '30's fictional Manhattan was
flooded with quaint calling cards and suave roguish
cracksmen were smirking from every penthouse. Popular
Publications had Captain Satan, who began his career
early in 1938. What the Captain left around as a trademark was the mark of Satan, "a device cut out of some
material like black felt—a round, horned head with a
hooked nose, and a clawed hand holding a tined pitchfork
aloft." Captain Satan was actually playboy Cary Adair,
who had as a friend powerful, sturdy Jo Desher, chief of
the Federal Bureau of Investigation. Desher doesn't know

his playboy friend is fond of slipping into black clothes and black rubber soled shoes and taking the law into his own hands. Desher is usually in the need of a little outside help. For instance, in "The Mask Of The Damned," he has to contend not only with deranged baseball players but with the fact that "official Washington is slowly going crazy!" The Captain Satan magazine didn't last long and in its last days the Captain had changed into a member of the police department.

Phantom ladies were less frequent than male avengers. Among the few practicing in an essentially masculine field was the Domino Lady. She appeared momentarily in the mid 1930's in *Mystery Adventure Magazine*. Ellen Patrick is the daytime name of Domino Lady and this is how she got interested in avenging:

> Her father had been one of the most feared politicians in California at one time. A killer's slug had put a period to his career several years before, and rumor had it that the assassin had been in the employ of Owen Patrick's crooked political enemies. A small trust fund, and a wealth of spirit and wit had been the lovely Ellen's heritage from her father.
>
> Accustomed to a life of ease as befitted the only child of Owen Patrick, Ellen had graduated at Berkeley, and was vacationing in the Far East when news of her father's assassination came to her. Dashing homeward in a heartbroken daze, she had sworn vengeance ... For three years now, she had pursued the life of a ruthless, roguish adventuress, at times accepting nigh impossible undertakings simply for the sake of friendship and the love of adventure.

Beyond doubt she was the most attractive of the phantom crimefighters. Lars Anderson, the nominal author of the novels, described her thus: "There is no gainsaying that the girl was perfectly beautiful. A jaunty black hat partially covered a cap of sun-touched curls which gleamed like molten gold . . . A cape of black silk was drawn about bare, milk-white shoulders. Beneath the folds of the cape, a backless frock of white silk sheathed her lovely body like a glove! It was daringly cut, and accentuated the exposed loveliness of her swollen bosom, and added a nimbus of sweet allure to the perfect picture of feminine pulchritude! A shining domino mask of black silk partly covered the lovely features. To any law enforcement officer in California the costume would readily have identified the beautiful intruder as that daring mysterious creature, *The Domino Lady!"*

A late entrant into the masked marvel competition was the Green Lama, who made his debut in the April, 1940 issue of *Double Detective*. This magazine, one of the declining Munsey line, had been around since 1937. It had featured a Complete Mystery Novel plus a batch of novelets and short stories, with most of the material in the politely hardboiled style all the Munsey detective pulps then favored. The Lama's premier novel-length adventure was titled "The Case Of The Crimson Hand" and Richard Foster was credited as author. Richard Foster was actually Kendall Foster Crossen, who was editing *Detective Fiction Weekly* for the Munsey outfit at the time. "The Green Lama came into existence in a sort of off-hand manner," Crossen told me. *"Double Detective* wasn't doing too well and they wanted to flesh it up. . . . It was finally decided to do something to compete with The Shadow and I was asked to draw up an outline for such a character. The result was the Green Lama (first called the Gray Lama but changed for reasons of color on the cover) and I was asked to write it."

Like The Shadow, the Lama had several alternate identities. The Shadow would sometimes be wealthy playboy Lamont Cranston and the Green Lama would sometimes show up around Manhattan as wealthy playboy Jethro

Dumont. Perhaps they even attended the same elite society affairs. Dumont, as was frequently observed in the footnotes accompanying the novels, "had fallen heir to a fortune estimated at ten million dollars while still at Harvard. It was during his college days that he first became interested in the Oriental religions. Shortly after his graduation he went to Tibet and studied for several years, later becoming a fully ordained priest in the Lamaist sect of Buddhism. He then returned to America and took up residence on Park Avenue." When he was being Dumont, the Lama had the mandatory Oriental servant. Crossen apparently studied Dorothy Lamour movies as well as Buddhism and the Lama's servant was named Tsarong. Another of the Green Lama's cover personalities was that of Dr. Pali, the name deriving from the name for the sacred language of the early Buddhist writings. With the aid of his small makeup kit the Lama was able to assume "the ruddy, moon-like" face the Dr. Pali role called for. In this phase he wore a dark green suit, light green ecclesiastical shirt and turned collar, somewhat resembling an offcolor Catholic priest. When he was appearing as the Green Lama himself he wore a green hood and robe over his other clothes, with a braided hair ring in the six sacred colors on the middle finger of his right hand. Around his neck he wore a dark red *kava,* or scarf, which was his only weapon. Most of his changes of persona usually serve no function in the stories and it is never made clear, even with footnotes, exactly why the Green Lama needs all these alternate identities. Perhaps simply Dumont's desire to keep up with the Cranstons.

Another relatively short-lived avenger was Jim Anthony, the Super Detective. He began his mystery man career just before World War II in *Super-Detective* magazine, a pulp published by Frank Armer's Trojan Publishing Corp. Armer had already gained distinction in the pulp field with such magazines as *Spicy Detective* and

Spicy Adventure. A blurb explained the Super Detective this way: "A strange man is Jim Anthony! Strange indeed! A man who can never be fully understood even by his best friends! Being the son of a Comanche princess and a world-famous Irish adventurer and millionaire, he has inherited remarkable characteristics—mental, physical and psychical!" Anthony's was not the most frightening of costumes. He did his Super Detective work wearing yellow swim trunks and a pair of Indian moccasins. The penname on the Jim Anthony novels was John Grange. The stories were a collaboration between Robert Leslie Bellem and W.T. Ballard, two prolific writers of detective fiction whose other work we'll look at in a later chapter. "Bob Bellem and I wrote the character from its inception until I left California for Wright Field during the war," Ballard explained to me. "At the same time we were also doing a series about a Chinese. Doctor Somebody. I can't for the life of me recall the name. . . . The stuff was pure formula and I did most of it on a dictaphone. I could dictate anywhere from thirty to forty pages a day."

CHAPTER SIX

DOC SAVAGE AND HIS CIRCLE

Recently it had occurred to Doc Savage he might be turning into too much of a machine—becoming, in fact, as superhuman as many persons thought he was. He did not like that idea. He had always been apprehensive lest something of the kind occur. The scientists who had trained him during his childhood had been afraid of his losing human qualities; they had guarded him against this as much as possible. When a man's entire life is fantastic, he must guard against his own personality becoming strange.

—Kenneth Robeson,
The Dagger In The Sky

YOU never know what sort of monument you'll get or what you'll be remembered for. Lester Dent had hoped to have a chance to write what he felt were first rate books and stories, the kind of thing that shows up on slick paper and best seller lists. Instead he got hired to write the Doc

Savage series and he spent nearly two decades hidden behind the penname Kenneth Robeson. The current Bantam paperback revivals of the old Doc Savage novels have now sold over twelve million copies and so Dent has become, some ten years after his death, one of the best selling authors of the century.

The official version of the inception of Doc Savage is that the entire concept was originated by Henry W. Ralston of Street & Smith. More probably, the character developed out of the numerous conferences on new titles which followed the unexpected success of The Shadow. "The Shadow was going so good, it fooled hell out of everybody," recalls Walter Gibson. "Ralston wanted to start another adventure magazine, but for a long time he didn't even have a title." John Nanovic, who edited both *The Shadow* and the new *Doc Savage* magazines, was also in on the planning of the new series. Basically the Doc Savage format—that of a strong and brilliant hero and his coterie of gifted and whimsical sidekicks—is Frank Merriwell and his chums updated. And there were numerous other successful gangs of fictional do-gooders around in the 1920's and '30's that might have served as inspiration, especially Edgar Wallace's Four Just Men. Street & Smith might even have noticed a series one of their own authors was doing over at Fiction House. A year before the debut of Doc, Theodore Tinsley was writing novelets about a manhunter named Major Lacy, who had his headquarters in "the towering pinnacle of the Cloud building" and was aided by a variously gifted quartet of his ex-Marine buddies. Clark Gable influenced the development of Doc, too. When artist Walter Baumhofer was called in to paint the cover for the first issue of *Doc Savage Magazine* he was handed this description of the character: "A Man of Bronze—known as *Doc,* who looks very much like Clark Gable. He is so well built that the impression is not of size, but of power." Baumhofer ignored this and made Doc look like the model he was using at the moment. In the stories, of course, Doc's full name is Clark Savage.

When he took on the Doc Savage job in 1933, Lester Dent was in his early thirties and already a prolific writer of pulp stories. A contemporary describes him as being then "a huge, red-headed man, six feet three and weighing around two hundred pounds." Dent grew up on his family's farm in La Plata, Missouri and despite his later wanderings he continued to refer to himself as "just a Missouri hillbilly." In the mid 1930's, writing about himself in the third person for a publicity release, Dent depicted his early years this way:

As a small boy, Lester Dent was taken across Wyoming in a covered wagon. Six weeks were required for a trip which can be made by automobile today in three hours.

Dent lived as a youth on a Wyoming cow ranch. Also lived on a farm near La Plata, Mo.

Dent was nineteen years old before his hair was ever cut by a barber.

Dent has only a High School education, but he attended Chillicothe Business College, learned to telegraph, and went to work for $45.00 a month.

Dent studied law nights.

While working a night telegraph job—from midnight until eight in the morning—Dent turned his hand to writing adventure stories. His first thirteen stories, nobody would buy. The fourteenth story sold for $250.00.

A few months later, a large New York publishing house, after reading the first story Dent sent them, telegraphed him to the effect that, "If you make less than a hundred dollars a week on your present job, advise you to quit; come to New York and be taken under our wing, with a five-hundred-dollar-a-month drawing account."

After telegraphing friends in New York to inquire around about the publisher's sanity, Dent went to New York. That was in 1931.

The publisher who called Dent away from his As-
sociated Press job in Tulsa was Dell. He wrote stories for
their *War Aces, War Birds, All Western, Western Romances* and *All Detective.* He eventually wrote for many
of the other pulp outfits and had sold to Street & Smith's
Popular and *Top Notch* before taking up the Savage as-
signment. Though much of the pulp writing Dent did
sounds like the work of a man who is enjoying himself,
he often privately referred to it as "crud." Asked to ex-
plain Doc Savage to a reporter, Dent said, "He has the
clue-following ability of Sherlock Holmes, the muscular
tree-swinging ability of Tarzan, the scientific sleuthing of
Craig Kennedy and the morals of Jesus Christ."

The first issue of *Doc Savage Magazine* was dated
March, 1933, and sold for ten cents. The Baumhofer cover
showed a slightly tattered Doc standing in front of a piece
of Mayan ruin that had several sinister natives lurking
behind it. Baumhofer, who did every cover of the magazine for the next several years, has yet to read a Doc
Savage novel. He usually based his cover paintings on a
short synopsis provided by one of the art editors. He got
seventy-five dollars per oil painting. The interior illustrations were drawn by Paul Orban. Orban followed direc-
tions and so inside the new magazine Doc did indeed look
like Clark Gable for awhile. "I actually read all the stories," Orban told me. "The editors never interfered or
suggested what to draw. The artists were on their own.
. . . The going price was fifteen dollars a drawing and
thirty dollars for a double page spread." Unlike Baumhofer, who never encountered Lester Dent, Orban did
meet him once, though briefly.

The maiden Doc Savage adventure was titled "The
Man Of Bronze." This inaugural novel about Clark Savage, Jr. and his group is written in a breathless turgid
prose that is not characteristic of Dent and probably indi-
cates some editorial committee work. It begins, "There

was death afoot in the darkness," and ends, "The giant bronze man and his five friends would confront undreamed perils as the very depths of hell itself crashed upon their heads. And through all that, the work of Savage would go on!" In between the reader is introduced to Doc, who possesses "an unusually high forehead, a mobile and muscular, but not too-full mouth, lean cheeks." He looks like a statue sculptured in bronze, is what he looks like, and "most marvelous of all were his eyes. They glistened like pools of flake gold." He also has nice teeth. "This man was Clark Savage, Jr. Doc Savage! The man whose name was becoming a byword in the odd corners of the world!" This exclamatory novel also introduces Doc's crew of five. Here they are, walking into Doc's headquarters atop one of the tallest buildings in New York:

> The first of the five men was a giant who towered four inches over six feet. He weighted fully two fifty. His face was severe, his mouth thin and grim . . . This was "Renny" or Colonel John Renwick. . . . He was known throughout the world for his engineering accomplishments.
>
> Behind Renny came William Harper Littlejohn, very tall, very gaunt. . . . He was probably one of the greatest living experts on geology and archaeology.
>
> Next was Major Thomas J. Roberts, dubbed "Long Tom." Long Tom was the physical weakling of the crowd . . . He was a wizard with electricity.
>
> "Ham" trailed Long Tom. "Brigadier General Theodore Marley Brooks," Ham was designated on formal occasions. Slender, waspy, quick-moving . . . and possibly the most astute lawyer Harvard ever turned out.
>
> Last came the most remarkable character of all. Only a few inches over five feet tall, he weighed better than two hundred and sixty pounds. He had the build of a gorilla . . . "Monk!" No other name could fit him!

Besides looking like an ape, Monk is a chemical wizard.

The rest of the first novel details Doc's avenging the recent death of his father, exploring Mayan ruins in the Central American republic of Hidalgo, unmasking a villain known as the Feathered Serpent and finding enough gold to finance the remaining years of his pulp career.

In the issue after this came a lost world novel, "The Land Of Terror," and next a Southern swamp adventure, "Quest Of The Spider." As the series progressed a distinct Dent type of book developed. The dime novel aura which was present in the first stories faded and both the plots and the prose dropped much of their melodrama. Dent's sense of humor moved closer to the surface and by the mid 1930's the Doc Savage adventures had some resemblance to the screwball movies of the period. He was more and more mixing adventure and detective elements with wackiness and producing a sort of pulpwood equivalent of films like *The Thin Man, Gunga Din* and *China Seas.* These movies, despite different locales and themes, shared a fooling-around quality that was current then in a good many Hollywood pictures. In his Doc Savage novels Dent pushed the usual pulp adventure and science fiction plots often quite close to parody, whether he was dealing with infernal machines, plagues, master thieves, pixies or ogres. While quite a few of his competitors can now be read for their unconscious humor, all of the laughs in Dent are intentional. He excelled in devising villains who were both bizarre and baggy-pantsed. For instance:

> Off to one side was a child's crib. It was an elaborate thing, with carvings and gilt inlays, and here and there rows of pearl studding. . . . The crib was about four feet long. The man who occupied it had plenty of room. . . . He was a little gem of a man.
>
> His face had that utter handsomeness which pen-and-

ink artists give their heroes in the love story magazines. He wore little bathing trunks and a little bathrobe, smoked a little cigar in a little holder, and a toy glass on a rack at the side held a toy drink in which leaned a toy swizzle stick.

Dent was also partial to slender, salty tomboy heroines and they appear in most of the novels.

> The big eyes were blue, a nice shade. There was more about her that was nice, too. Her nose, the shape of her mouth. Long Tom had a weakness for slender girls, and this one was certainly slender. She wore stout leather boots, shorts, a khaki blouse and a khaki pith helmet.
> "Don't stand there staring!" she snapped. "I want a witness! Somebody to prove I saw it."

> She was a redhead. In height, she would have topped Doc's shoulder a bit. . . . Altogether her features could hardly have been improved upon. She wore an amazing costume —a loose, brocaded Russian blouse, drawn in at the waist with a belt fashioned of parallel lines of gold coins. From this dangled a slender, jewelled sword which Doc was certain dated back at least four centuries. There was also an efficent, spike-nosed, very modern automatic pistol.

Dent's action was often presented in choppy, quick-cut movie style. As in this assault from the novel, "Red Snow":

> Doc Savage put on speed. He came in sight of the basement window just in time to see the golf-hosed legs of his quarry disappearing inside. Then, in the basement, a man saw Doc and bellowed profanely. What might have been a thick-walled steel pipe of small diameter jutted out of the window. Its tip acquired a flickering red spear-point of flame. The weapon was an automatic rifle of military calibre and its roar volleyed through the compound.

Doc Savage had rolled behind a palm, which, after the fashion of palms when stunted, was extremely wide at the base. The tree shuddered, and dead leaves loosened and fluttered in the wind. A cupro-nickel-jacketed slug came entirely through the bole. More followed. The bole began to split. The racket was terrific.

He also worked out a distinctive and personal way of starting a story. These were often abrupt and unlike the usual slow and moody Street & Smith openings so much favored by writers like Walter Gibson. For example:

When Ethel's Mama blew up, she shook the earth in more ways than one.

When the plane landed on a farmer's oat-stubble field in the Mississippi bottoms near St. Louis, the time was around ten in the morning.
The farmer had turned his cattle on to the stubble field to graze, and among the animals was a rogue bull which was a horned devil with strangers.
The bull charged the aviator.
The flier killed the bull with a spear.

The street should be very clean. The long-faced man had been sweeping it since daylight.

Never completely reverent of Doc, Dent extemporized abilities for him that went beyond the wildest talents of your average everyday super-hero. In one novel, for instance, Doc Savage displays not only a remarkable knack for fashion designing but an exceptional skill for leading a dance band.

Doc Savage Magazine proved to be another best-selling title for Street & Smith and it stayed on the stands for sixteen years all told. The periodical remained monthly until after the war and then declined down through bi-monthly and finally quarterly publication. There were

181 separate novels devoted to Doc Savage, all credited to Kenneth Robeson. Of these Dent seems to have written all but about two dozen. The official Street & Smith records, now looked after by Conde Nast Publications, show nine Doc Savage novels are the work of the ubiquitous Norman Daniels, four are by Alan Hathway and three by William Bogart. All three men were S&S hacks in the '30's and '40's. Laurence Donovan, another undistinguished workhorse, is also sometimes mentioned as having contributed to the corpus. The major period of ghosting was in 1936 and 1937. According to Frank Gruber, "along about 1936 Lester Dent began to tire of Doc Savage. He thought the stories too juvenile and he thought that he should be trying to write more adult fiction." During these same years Dent acquired the forty-foot Albatross, which he referred to as his "treasure hunt schooner," and he was spending a good deal of time aboard it. Besides the ghost writers who made the official list at Street & Smith, Dent hired a few others on the side. Ryerson Johnson, an affable little pulp writer, remembers doing at least three Doc Savages in 1935. "I did 'Land Of Always Night,'" he told me. "Another one, and something about the Galapagos Islands and giant turtles." Dent made $750 per novel and he paid Johnson $500 out of that. Johnson remembers being handed $500 in cash on a street corner in Manhattan after doing the giant turtles book.

As a merchandising property Doc Savage didn't equal The Shadow. There were no movies, no serials. There was a radio show, but it ran only in the East during one wartime summer. The Doc Savage comic book never did well either. A number of cartoonists drew the feature, including William A. Smith, later a *Saturday Evening Post* illustrator and currently a gallery painter. As with many of their later characters, Street & Smith's timing was off. They didn't think of using him as a comic book hero until 1940 and by then there was Superman. It's obvious Jerry

Siegel and Joe Shuster had recognized Doc Savage's potential much earlier. Dedicated pulp readers, the two young Cleveland boys borrowed considerably from Dent's character for their own super-hero. It isn't because of coincidence that Superman's name is Clark Kent and that he was initially billed as the Man of Steel. In the pulp magazines themselves there were a number of imitation Docs. None of them, such as Captain Hazard, survived beyond the '30's. Street & Smith tried, too, most notably with a sea-faring adventurer named Cap Fury. The captain and his crew had their own magazine for awhile. It was called *The Skipper* and the busy Norman Daniels ghosted the novels.

Lester Dent died just ten years after his character had folded. That was in 1959 while he was, once more, on a treasure hunting cruise. A year prior to that Dent, who never substantially realized his ambition to progress to slicks and bestsellers, was asked to reminisce about his pulp days. He had by then written hundreds of short stories and nearly two hundred novels, earning as much as $4,000 a month. All he spoke well of out of all that material were the two short stories he'd done for *Black Mask* in the 1930's. He sold the stories, both of which dealt with a lean Florida detective named Sail, to editor Joseph Shaw. He admired Shaw for being "gentle with his writers. You went into *Black Mask* and talked with him, you felt you were doing fiction that was powerful, you had feelings of stature." In 1936 Shaw was fired from the magazine. This, Lester Dent felt, "is what kept me from becoming a fine writer. Had I been exposed to the man's cunning hand for another year or two, I couldn't have missed. . . . Instead I wrote reams of saleable crap which became my pattern, and gradually there slipped away the bit of power Shaw had started awakening in me."

CHAPTER SEVEN

SPECIAL AGENTS

The basic concept of Operator 5 was that he must save the United States from total destruction in every story, every month. When I was called in to start the series they already had a cover illustration . . . the White House being blown up.
—*Frederick C. Davis*

ALL the Federal Bureau of Investigation and the other government undercover agencies had to contend with in the '30's were John Dillinger, Machine Gun Kelly, Ma Barker, Baby Face Nelson and the spies Hitler sent over. In real life, anyway. In the pulps it was a much harder life and the occupational hazards were monumental. Next to the masked mystery men, nobody in the Depression years pulp magazines had more troubles than the spies and secret agents.

The special agent who coped with more unusual, un-

common, unprecedented and unparalleled problems
than anyone else was unquestionably Operator 5. Just the
titles of some of his cases would have scared the average
1930's G-Man off. It's not everybody who wants to tangle
with the "Winged Hordes of the Yellow Vulture," "Hell's
Yellow Legions," "Death's Call to Arms," "The Suicide
Battalion" and "The Army of the Dead." Operator 5 began
his career in the middle of the Depression in one of the
several Popular Publications which were extravagantly
alert to the possibility of foreign invasion. The complete
title of his magazine was *Secret Service Operator #5*,
with the subtitle *America's Undercover Ace*. Signed with
the forceful penname Curtis Steele, the Operator 5 novels
were initially by Frederick C. Davis. "The basic concept
of Operator 5 came from Harry Steeger, the publisher, or
Rogers Terrill, the editor, or both," recalled Davis when
I asked him about the character in 1969. "It was that
Operator 5 must save the United States from total destruction in every story, every month. When I was called
in to start the series they already had a cover illustration
. . . the White House being blown up. I did the first Operator 5 around this picture. The characters in detail, the
ideas, the plots and the gimmicks were all my inventions."

Operator 5 was actually handsome young Jimmy Christopher. "He was in his early twenties, yet there was an
unshakable confidence in his bearing that added dignity
to his years," is how he is described in the December,
1934, issue. "On the back of his right hand a scar shone.
It was a mark of black and white and gray which resem-
bled to an astonishing degree a spread-winged American
eagle. There was a tiny charm affixed to his watch-chain,
fashioned delicately of gold, a skull and crossbones with
eyes of ruby-red." A bit later Jimmy took to wearing a
skull ring as well. "An ordinary appearing ring to anyone
who did not know its secret—but beneath that skull lay

concealed a quantity of an explosive so powerful it could bring down an entire building." You could get yourself a handsome replica of this ring, minus the explosive charge, by sending ten cents to Operator 5.

Not only was Jimmy Christopher young and confident, he was unquestionably of the right stock. Here he is in July, 1935, walking past a hungry and angry mob near the White House:

> A young man strode quietly toward the edge of the growing crowd while the howl dinned in his ears. Clean-cut, sharp-eyed, alert, he paused to study those giving growling support to the inflammatory speaker. His face was that of an American, while in the mob were scores of faces of foreign cast. His features were finely turned, but among the hundreds were many faces that were evil and malevolent. He had a mind that functioned coolly, keenly; theirs were minds swayed by the florid eloquence of any speaker last to address them.
>
> They were a mere mob. He was the ace undercover agent of the United States Government.

Jimmy's boss is a man so secretive that few knew "that this man was the Commander-in-Chief of the United States Intelligence Service. To even his most trusted agents he was known only by the cryptic designation of Z-7." Another regular in the series was Diane Eliot. She was Jimmy Christopher's fiancee, "but they were far more than sweethearts. They had been welded more closely together by unselfish service to their country than the marriage vows they would some day take could ever make them." Also aiding Jimmy in his innumerable encounters with death and worse was Tim Donovan, "freckle-faced, pug-nosed, wiry young stripling." One other frequent visitor to the novels was Jimmy's haggard old father, ex-operator Q-6. Like many another master spy,

Jimmy Christopher was an expert at disguise. A knack he may well have picked up at his father's knee. Jimmy is almost never without his makeup, which he carries in a small black metal case. He also often wears a concealed sword. In the lulls between invasions he likes to do magic tricks to amuse young Tim.

In his first few pulp years Operator 5 faced a variety of bizarre threats. "It was he who almost single-handed stopped the attack on this country by Schreckites and prevented their use of plague-spreading germs which would have swept this nation with deadly diseases," boasted one of his colleagues once. "He commanded, over the general staff of the Army and Navy, the counterattack which defeated the Asiatic invasion of Alaska." As the 1930's drew to a close Jimmy Christopher came to devote himself exclusively to the Japanese. What had happened was that "political scheming had transformed the United States into three warring, hostile camps—and the Asiatic invader had used this opportunity to strike the deathblow!" By the spring of 1939 things had turned quite bad. "Over America's great West swept eerie death-clouds that had been loosed by an incredible invasion of Asiatic robots!" Besides which "our helpless citizens were overwhelmed by the inhuman leper-scourge." Not to mention the fact that there were "hundreds—no, thousands—of Japanese there in the middle of South Dakota!" Masterminding all this is Moto Taronago, whose predatory countenance and vulturine profile have, when coupled with his sadistic ways, earned him the nickname of the Yellow Vulture.

Operator 5 went out of business after the real war with the Japanese began. Frederick Davis had abandoned him sometime earlier. "I don't remember how long I kept Operator 5 going . . . several years anyway. Eventually it got to be just too much."

The Thrilling entrant in the special agent field appeared in their *G-Men Detective* magazine. He was "tall, broad-shouldered, and wore well cut civilian clothes. He gave the impression—and correctly—that beneath the tweeds were muscles as supple and strong as those beneath the silken hide of a jungle cat. But he was far more than a man who was superbly fit physically. He was a man whose brain, razor-sharp, could instantly pounce on the slightest clue in any case he might take over in his capacity as F.B.I. inspector, and interpret the most obscure meanings. He was a man, too, of undaunted courage, of fearlessness in the face of danger. He was, in fact, Dan Fowler, greatest ace of the F.B.I." J. Edgar Hoover, though referred to only as the Director, was a regular in the Dan Fowler adventures. There was no penname attached to the series and whoever batted out an episode got to sign his name to it. For ten cents you could join Dan Fowler's G-Men Club.

Over at Ace they had Secret Agent X, many of whose problems were alliterative. Every other month he had to worry about such things as "Satan's Syndicate," "Slaves of the Scorpion," "Corpse Contraband" and "The Curse of the Crimson Horde." X was not exactly a G-Man and "his name, if he had one, was unknown. That was exactly as he preferred it. . . . He preferred to be known simply as Secret Agent X. And while he was closely allied with the men of the F.B.I., and sponsored by a powerful Washington official, his unorthodox methods of crime detection had so frequently carried him into lawless shadows that he had been branded a desperate criminal." Like many of his spy contemporaries X was very good at disguise. "Secret Agent X's ability as an impersonator is a combination of superlative voice mimicry, character acting that great Thespians might well envy, and a sculptor-like skill in molding plastic material over his own features so that they resemble those of another man." X's relatively brief ca-

reer was a mixture of slam-bang action and sultry encounters, done up in hothouse prose, with exotic women:

> X had to make a quick choice. One of the Mongols was
> in an excellent position to knife him from the rear. But
> across the room, another had come to grips with the red-
> headed girl. X thought of himself last and delayed his
> move for self preservation long enough to shoot a leg out
> from under the yellow man who was trying to knife the
> redhead.
>
> Instantly X dropped almost to all fours in time to catch
> the Mongol who sprang from behind him, by means of a
> body-block which threw the yellow man heels over head.
> ... The Agent sprang toward the two Mongols who seemed
> to be guarding the masked man. If he could but lay the
> leader by the heels the whole elaborate and deadly scheme
> of the cult might be defeated. The two Mongols parted
> suddenly before X's onrush.
>
> Directly behind the point where X expected to find the
> masked leader, there was a closed door. Then he heard the
> redhead's frantic cry: *"Art!"*
>
> The girl sprang to the right and at the same time drew a
> gun from the folds of her dark gown. But X leaped at the
> same time, seizing her in his arms, crushing her gun hand
> against her own chest. He held her a moment.
>
> "Pull the trigger, Erlika, and save the hangman a very
> unpleasant task."
>
> She spat at his face. "Son of a pig!" she snarled. "Release
> me. I am the daughter of Erlik."
>
> "You are a very beautiful, completely spoiled,
> thoroughly wicked woman," he said with a laugh.
>
> She raised her head suddenly, and her teeth snapped at
> his throat.

Signed with the openly fake name Brant House, the Secret Agent X novels were supposedly turned out by several men.

Operator 5 and Secret Agent X were not the only spies with bizarre caseloads. Equaling them was the Master American Flying Spy, G-8. From 1933 through 1944, G-8 went up against everything from "batlike monsters, their eyes fire, their breath a poison vapor" to "bombs piloted by living beast men." All the novels of World War I espionage and air battles that appeared in the *G-8 and His Battle Aces* magazine were written by Robert J. Hogan. Hogan, who died in the mid-1960's, had learned to fly during World War I while an air cadet with the Signal Corps. After that he flew and sold airplanes for Curtiss-Wright and finally in 1930 tried pulp writing. In 1933, Harry Steeger of Popular Publications decided to try a book-length aviation novel and G-8 resulted. "The publishers and editors had no part in the G-8 form," recalls Hogan's widow, Betty Nevin. "They merely made the original suggestion he write a full-length series. Since he had been writing mostly air stories, it was taken for granted that they would be air novels. I don't know how the fantastic angle came about. I think most of it was developed the first time the idea of a series was discussed. I know he was driving home from New York and worked out the first novel, *The Bat Staffel.* He felt a full-length series might bog down without stronger, fantastic-type plots."

While G-8 was flying the unfriendly skies of World War I, Dusty Ayres was looking after the future. Dusty, often called the Top Eagle of Uncle Sam's Brood, began in 1933 to fight the Next Great War. The recurring problem faced by Dusty Ayres and his Battle Birds was the Blacks. "In Central Asia it had found its beginning. From out of that whirlpool of mixed bloods had arisen a man of mystery —a figure who was soon to become know as Fire-Eyes, Emperor of the World. No one had ever seen his face, for it was always covered with a green mask, perfectly blank save for two slits through which orbs of sparkling flame looked out on the world. The rest of his body, every single part of it, was covered by a black uniform. . . . Without warning, his fierce and cruel armies, who became known as the Black Invaders, had started sweeping across the world, crushing everything that civilized man had built up since the beginning of time. In three years all Europe and Asia was ground beneath the iron hell of Fire-Eyes. And next—the greatest nation of all, the United States of America."

Dusty usually flew in a plane named the Silver Flash, "his one and only sky pal." Once up there he took on the best the Blacks had to offer and his particular nemesis was the Invader ace known only as the Black Hawk. On the ground the Hawk was given to smirking and gloating but once in the sky there was nothing effete about the man. After many encounters Dusty, in a novel entitled "The Purple Tornado," finally rids the airways of him:

Through red-filmed eyes Dusty saw the Hawk turn in the seat and look back. A split second later the Black plane cut sharply to the left and went streaking out across Long Island. Dusty laughed harshly and tore after him.

"No you don't!" he bellowed. "This time I deal the cards. Here, blast you, this is for Billings!"

Hot steel from his guns slashed into the tail of the other ship. It lurched crazily to the right. Like a flash Dusty was on it again.

"And this for Major Walker!"

Desperately the Hawk tried to skid clear, but Dusty's singing steel caught him square amidships. The Black plane reeled over on its wing. Then it spun around in a dime turn and charged straight for him, guns spitting flame.

Oblivious to the blazing fire from the other's guns, Dusty held his ship dead-on for the whirling prop. His eyes gleamed like balls of fire as he saw his bursts crash into the other plane.

It was the Hawk who finally weakened and cut away to avoid a mid-air crash. And that moment was the supreme climax of Dusty's entire life. He flung his ship down to the right. . . . Clinging to the tail of the Black ship, Dusty poured burst after burst into it. And then, when the Black ship was but a bare hundred feet off the ground, the right wing let go, and the plane went cartwheeling crazily off to the right. Seconds later it became lost to view in a great cloud of smoky dust, as it hit on the edge of a small field.

The Dusty Ayres novels were the work of Robert Sidney Bowen. He came by his flying experience first hand, having been with the Royal Air Force in the First World War. Before turning to fulltime pulp writing in 1931, he had been editor of *Aviation Magazine.* When I asked Bowen, who now lives in Hawaii, how Dusty Ayres came about, he replied: "Frankly, it was a spur of the moment thing that Harry Steeger and I cooked up one day in 1933 when we were having lunch together. It was this way, as near as I can remember it. At the time I was turning out some one hundred and fifty yarns a year of all types and lengths. War-Air stories, gangland stories, mystery stories, sports stories, detective stories, adventure stories, and what have you. And I was sort of tired of banging out one kind of story one day and another kind the next. Anyway, I happened to mention to Harry that I'd like to do a whole magazine a month like Bob Hogan was doing. And Harry said, 'Okay, let's think up something.' Well, naturally I didn't want to do a mag that would be in direct competition with Bob's, so that type was out. Well, Harry and I tossed ideas at each other during the rest of the lunch and came up with the idea of an air-war magazine but about a war in the future. Of course it wouldn't be wise to write about a war in the future between the U.S. and some other country in the world. So we decided to make the enemy a bunch that rose up out of darkest Eastern Asia and started to conquer the world. I took it from there and doped out the series and wrote it."

Not all pulps bothered to think up a mythical invader and in the 1930's the Yellow Peril made a strong comeback. In 1912, the Manchu Dynasty, which had ruled China since the 17th Century, was overthrown. That same year in London former bank teller Arthur Sarsfield Ward was looking for something to call the sinister Oriental scientist he'd just thought up. He named him Dr. Fu Manchu and the Yellow Peril immediately took a great leap forward. By 1913, Ward, who wrote as Sax Rohmer, had enough short stories about the evil doctor to put together a book. The book appeared in the United States under the title *The Insidious Dr. Fu Manchu.* Narrated by a Watson-like Dr. Petrie, it deals with a series of encounters between the sinister doctor and handsome British detective and secret agent Nayland Smith. Smith believes he is working "not in the interest of the British government merely, but in the interests of the entire white race." When asked to describe the fiend he seeks, Smith grimly replies, "Imagine a person, tall, lean and feline, high-shouldered, with a brow like Shakespeare and a face like Satan, a close-shaven skull, and long magnetic eyes of the true cat-green. Invest him with all the cruel cunning of an entire Eastern race, accumulated in one giant intellect, with all the resources of science past and present, with all the resources, if you will, of a wealthy government—which, however, already had denied all knowledge of his existence. Imagine that awful being, and you have a mental picture of Dr. Fu Manchu, the yellow peril incarnate." Although Sax Rohmer's stories ran not on pulpwood but in slick paper magazines such as *Collier's*, this pre-war statement of policy was to influence generations of pulp writers, movie producers and serial performers. Not to mention members of our State Department.

When the Japanese invaded Manchuria in 1931, the Yellow Peril became a popular topic again. Several pulp magazines reflected the fear and the Fu Manchu villain was once again a staple. Another, and possibly more immediate, influence on the pulp publishers was the continued and still expanding success of the insidious doctor himself. Starting in 1929, Warner Oland made three profitable talkies as Fu Manchu. In 1932, MGM cast Boris Karloff in *The Mask of Fu Manchu.* Rohmer's character was also featured in a radio series throughout the '30's. All of this had an especially strong effect on Harry Steeger and Popular Publications. In the middle 1930's they tried two sinister Oriental pulps.

The first was *Wu Fang*, a very close imitation of Fu Manchu. The early issues of this pulp were even illustrated by John R. Flanagan, who had illustrated several of Fu Manchu's magazine and hardcover appearances. The Wu Fang novels were written by the prolific Robert J. Hogan. Hogan's version of the sinister Oriental looked like this: "He was a perfect personification of this title, Dragon Lord of Crime. He was tall and gaunt with sloping shoulders. His mouth was pinched and narrow, but the upper part of his face above the hideously gleaming green eyes widened to a forehead of great brain capacity." Hogan paraphrased not only Sax Rohmer's descriptions but his plots. In the Wu Fang saga the chief pursuer was Val Kildare, "former number one investigator of the United States Secret Service." Kildare was aided by Rod Carson, "eminent young explorer and archeologist." Robert Hogan's widow told me, "Wu Fang didn't last long. I can't remember much about it now, but I do remember we celebrated when it was decided to discontinue it."

Popular gave the Asian menace one more go-round in the summer of 1936 with a new pulp called *Dr. Yen Sin.* The premier issue utilized a leftover Wu Fang cover by Jerome Rozen and included short stories by Frank Gruber and Arch Oboler. The "smashing complete novel of Oriental menace" was by Donald E. Keyhoe. A decade and a half later Keyhoe, by then an ex-Air Force major, would scare the nation again. With a non-fiction work, *The Flying Saucers Are Real.* In 1936 he was content to worry about a simple terrestrial invasion. The insidious Dr. Yen Sin had come, according to the editorial message, "out of the teeming turbulent East . . . bringing to the capital of the West all the ancient Devil's-lore at his command— and a horde of Asian hell-born to help him spawn it." Yes, Dr. Yen Sin was in Washington, D.C., and up to no good. The first person to get a good look at him sees something "like a living picture of Satan. A yellow face looked out at him. He had a dazed glimpse of the Crime Lord's terrible smile—of that hideous face." The inventive Keyhoe made Yen Sin's eyes "tawny yellow" and not the traditional cat-green.

The white hope in the Yen Sin series is Michael Traile, also known as The Man Who Never Sleeps. Because of a childhood brain operation performed on him by an inept Hindu doctor, Traile literally never sleeps. This gives him a lot of extra time to track Dr. Yen Sin and to read up on arcane matters. He is assisted in his pursuit by young Eric Gordon, who smokes a pipe. Traile's is not an easy quest. He is beset frequently by Eastern stranglers, death rays, exotic lady spies and he can't always count on the kind of cooperation he'd like. When he requests that the Secretary of State look into the Yen Sin conspiracy, for example, the only reply he gets is, "I've already made inquiries at the Chinese Legation. They've never heard of Yen Sin and they ridiculed the idea of this 'Invisible Empire' which has you upset." The editorial in the first issue of *Dr. Yen Sin* expressed optimism about the public acceptance of this new magazine of "good Chinese fiction." The optimism was ill founded.

The Phantom Detective, October, 1935. Reprinted by permission of Popular Library Publishers.

Black Book Detective, Spring, 1944. Cover by Rudolph Belarski.
Reprinted by permission of Popular Library Publishers.

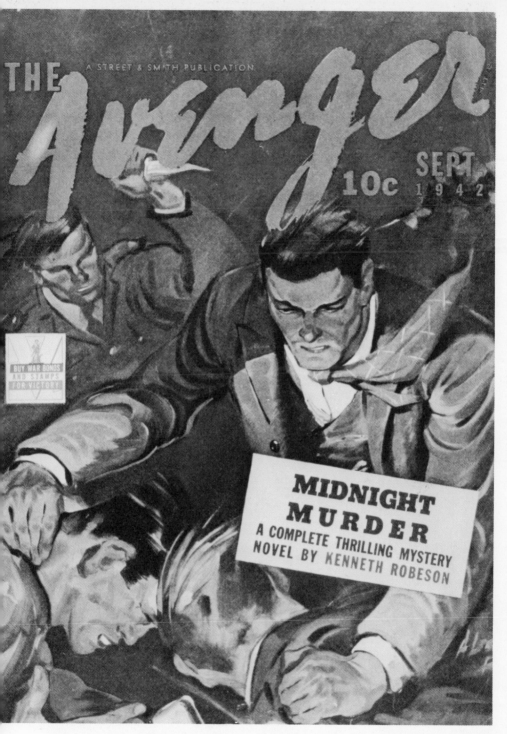

Avenger, September, 1942. Cover by A. Leslie Ross. From *Avenger,* copyright © 1942 by Street & Smith Publications, Inc.

CRIME BUSTERS

GREAT DETECTIVE STORIES

STREET & SMITH PUBLICATION

THE DEATH MOTH

COMPLETE MYSTERY NOVEL

By NORVELL PAGE

10¢

AUG. 1939

ALSO · DENT · TINSLEY · BALLARD · HARPER   AND OTHERS · ALL STORIES COMPLETE

Crime Busters, August, 1939. Cover by Hubert Rogers. From *Crime Busters,* copyright © 1939 by Street & Smith Publications, Inc.

"Slug him again!" said the punk as she flailed out with her slipper.

Hollywood Detective, August, 1950. Illustration by Max Plaisted, from page 17. The story: "Murder Wears Makeup."

Doc Savage, Monk and Ham. Illustrations by Paul Orban. From *Doc Savage Magazine,* copyright © 1934 by Street & Smith Publications, Inc.

Doc Savage Magazine, March, 1934. Cover by Walter Baumhofer. From *Doc Savage Magazine,* copyright © 1934 by Street & Smith Publications, Inc.

Doc Savage Magazine, April, 1934. Cover by Walter Baumhofer. From *Doc Savage Magazine,* copyright © 1934 by Street & Smith Publications, Inc.

LONG HAS THE LURE OF PIRATE
GOLD STIRRED THE HEARTS OF
MEN...LONG HAVE MEN FOUGHT AND
KILLED TO GAIN THE ILL-GOTTEN
WEALTH THAT THE PLUNDERERS OF
THE SEA BURIED YEARS AGO....ON
SUCH A QUEST DOES OUR STORY
TAKE US....ALTHOUGH WHEN THE
SEARCH FOR THE GOLD STARTED,
DOC SAVAGE AND HIS AIDES LITTLE
KNEW OF— THE BLACK KNIGHT...
WHO WAS TO CHALLENGE EVEN THE SA-
CRED POWERS OF DOC SAVAGE'S FAMOUS HOOD

Doc Savage Comics, September, 1943. Cover by William A.
Smith. From *Doc Savage Comics,* copyright © 1943 by
Street & Smith Publications, Inc.

Clues Detecitve Stories, November, 1935. Cover by Tom Lovell. From *Clues Detective Stories,* copyright © 1935 by Street & Smith Publications, Inc.

Blue Book, September, 1935. Cover by Herbert Morton Stoops.

NOW 10¢ PER COPY

THRILLING ADVENTURES

SEPT.

NOW 10¢

A THRILLING PUBLICATION

FEATURING

RIVER OF DEATH

A Complete Novel o
New Guinea's Headhunter

By COLONE
WILLIAM T
COWIN

GOLDEN HELL

An Amazing True Experience
By CAPTAIN HUMBERT REYNOLDS

THE DEVIL'S HOOF

A Novelette of Aleutian Piracy
By HERMAN HOWARD MATTESON

Thrilling Adventures, September, 1936. Cover by Rudolph Belarski.
Reprinted by permission of Popular Library Publishers.

Western Story, March 10, 1934. Cover by Fred Craft. From *Western Story,* copyright © 1934 by Street & Smith Publications, Inc.

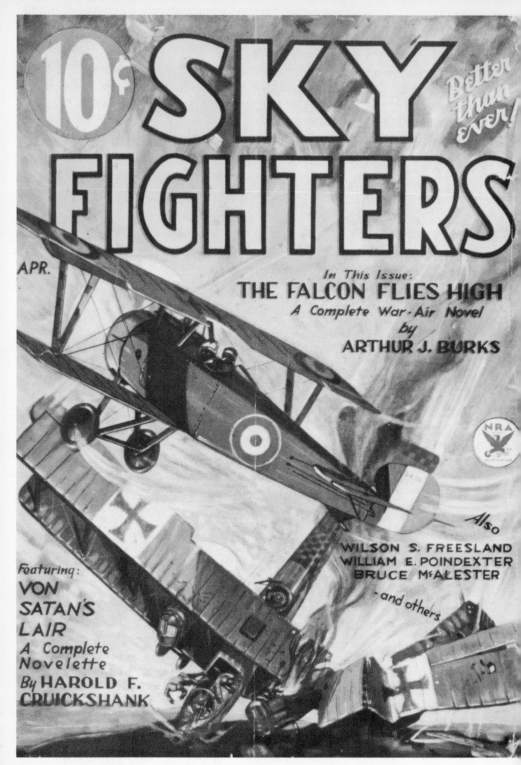

Sky Fighters, April, 1934. Reprinted by permission of Popular Library Publishers.

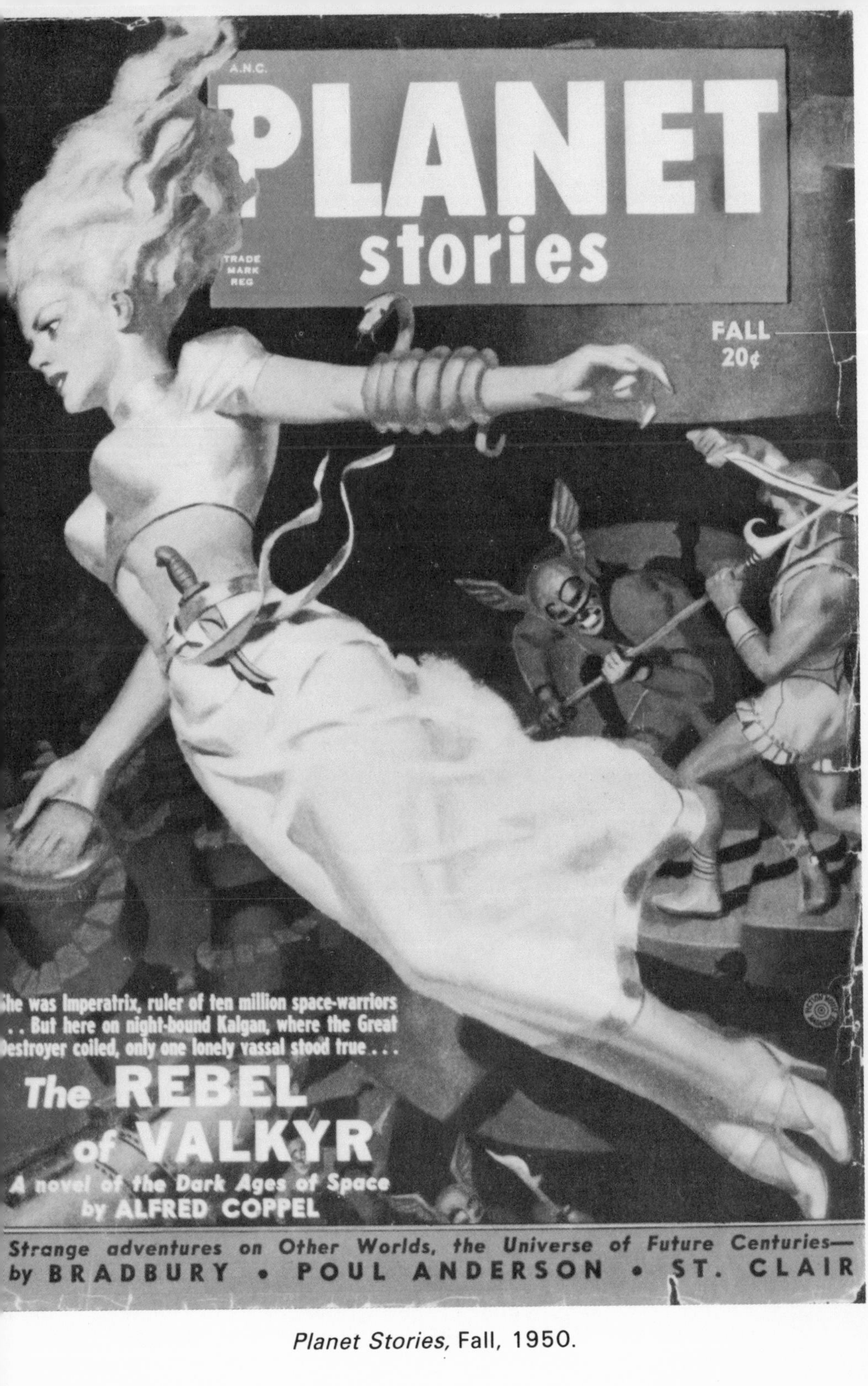

Planet Stories, Fall, 1950.

STREET & SMITH'S
WILD WEST .
15¢ WEEKLY
CONTENTS COPYRIGHTED 1934
AUG. II
ALL STORIES COMPLETE

THE RAID ON RAGTOWN
A "SILVER JACK STEELE"
NOVELETTE
BY WILLIAM
F. BRAGG

Blue Book, March, 1936. Illustration by Austin Briggs, from page 39. The story: "Shock Troops of Justice."

Blue Book, May, 1939. Illustration by John R. Flanagan, from page 71. The story: "Trumpets From Oblivion."

Astounding Science Fiction, November, 1949. Illustration by Edd Cartier, from page 155. From *Astounding Science Fiction,* copyright © 1949 by Street & Smith Publications, Inc.

The Shadow, scourge of the underworld, nemesis of crime, blasting his way through the evil machinations of master minds to justice! Mystery and action, packed with suspense and thrills, in every issue. A complete book-length novel; short detective stories, codes, crime problems, and other features pack every issue of this powerful mystery magazine

CHAPTER EIGHT

DIME DETECTIVES

It was rather a kind of meaningful violence, sometimes an explicit description and implicit criticism of a corrupt society. Many Americans lost faith in the society of the 1920's, and Hammett's heroes tried both to expose the corruptness and to speak for men who, questioning the values of society, needed to be assured that somewhere—if only on the pages of a pulp magazine—there were heroes who cared.
—*Philip Durham*

TOWARD the end of his life, Joseph T. Shaw, former Army captain and then literary agent, began to put together an anthology of detective stories. Though he eventually sold the book, entitled *The Hard-boiled Omnibus*, Shaw had a difficult time with it. This was in 1946, and there wasn't much interest that hopeful and forward-looking year in the dead and gone period when Shaw had been editor of a pulp magazine called *Black Mask*. Shaw persisted, believing something important had happened in the decade he was with the magazine. He did not claim credit for what had happened, but he was pleased to have been around when it did. During the years 1926 to 1936 the hardboiled detective story had grown up and been perfected in the pages of *Black Mask*. It was in the course of these years that Dashiell Hammett's *The Maltese Falcon, Red Harvest,* and *The Glass Key* appeared as serials in *Black Mask*. Raymond Chandler's first stories, the bases of the novels *The Big Sleep* and *Farewell, My Lovely,* were published in this same span of years. As was the work of Erle Stanley Gardner, George Harmon Coxe, Frederick Nebel, Lester Dent and Horace McCoy. And it was in these years and in this magazine that the private eye first became an important American hero.

The private eye was born in the early 1920's and flourished in the decades between the two World Wars. The private eye could only have happened first in those years after World War I, the years of Prohibition. There had always been aggressive, straight-shooting fiction heroes. But it took the mood of the '20's to add cynicism, detachment, a kind of guarded romanticism and a compulsion toward action. The disillusionment that followed the war, the frustration over the mushrooming gangster control of the cities affected the detective story as much as it did mainstream fiction. The same things began to unsettle the private detectives that bothered the heroes of Hemingway, Dos Passos and Fitzgerald. And the 1920's' preoccupation with the American language, the dissatisfaction with Victorian rhetoric and polite exposition was nowhere more strongly felt than among the writers of private eye stories. The new private detectives of the pulps, while varied individuals, shared certain attitudes and qualifications. They usually stayed away from small towns, most of them working for detective agencies or on their own in the large cities. New York, Chicago, Detroit,

Miami and Los Angeles, which *Black Mask* called the New Wild West. They shared, many of the private eyes, a distrust of the police and politicians. They could patiently collect evidence, but they could also cut corners the way the law couldn't. Yet they were linked with reality, with the real crimes of the urban world and the real smell and feel of the mean streets, and this put the best of them in a different class than the essentially adolescent phantom avengers. They were sometimes drunk, oftentimes broke. A private eye would always help somebody in trouble, though he would downplay his compassion. "I could have walked away. I started to walk away and then the sucker instinct got the best of me and I went back." Taking action was important, even if it wasn't well planned always. Though the private eye was not always hopeful, he stuck to his word. "It wasn't worth it, but then it was a deal."

The *Black Mask* magazine was started because H. L. Mencken needed money. Mencken and his literary accomplice, George Jean Nathan, had become co-editors and co-owners of *The Smart Set* magazine during World War I. Subtitled *A Magazine Of Cleverness, The Smart Set* printed high class fiction and pieces and was usually in a shaky financial position. Early in 1919 Mencken wrote to his friend, Ernest Boyd, "I am thinking of venturing into a new cheap magazine scheme, and if I do it will tie me to New York all summer. The opportunity is good and I need the money." Mencken and Nathan had already been involved with a couple of other pulps. These were *Saucy Stories* and *Parisienne,* both of which drew on *The Smart Set* reject pile for their material. In the case of *Parisienne* the stories were edited so they all had French settings. After turning down the opportunity to do an all-Negro pulp, Mencken and Nathan finally decided they'd try a mystery magazine. By this time Street & Smith's *Detective Story* magazine was a proven success.

Mencken named the new thriller *The Black Mask*. This title may have come to him while looking at the cover of *The Smart Set*, which each month featured a line drawing of a black masked Satan in its left hand corner. *The Black Mask* made its debut early in 1920. By April, sales were looking good, though Mencken still hated the magazine. "Our new louse, the *Black Mask,* seems to be a success," he said in a letter. "The thing has burdened both Nathan and me with disagreeable work."

Actually most of the early editorial work seems to have been done by Wyndham Martyn and Florence Osborne, associate editors on *The Smart Set.* The early issues of *The Black Mask* also drew on the office slush pile. Mencken and Nathan never allowed their names to appear on the pages of the new louse and Miss Osborne, under the more masculine sounding name of F.M. Osborne, was listed as the first editor. As the magazine's circulation climbed toward a quarter of a million copies a month, Mencken grew no fonder of it. *"The Black Mask* is a lousy magazine—all detective stories," he complained. "I hear that Woodrow reads it. Reading mss. for it is a fearful job, but it has kept us alive during a very bad year." While the magazine was still quite young Mencken and Nathan sold it, for something like one hundred thousand dollars. They'd started it with a cash outlay of five hundred dollars. One of their partners in the *Smart Set* venture, Eltinge Warner, stayed with *Black Mask* as business manager. Warner, who had made a success of *Field & Stream,* remained at *Black Mask* until 1940. Like Mencken, he thought little of detective stories and the writer he liked least was Dashiell Hammett.

Although one of Mencken's favorite topics, in both *The Smart Set* and, later, *The American Mercury,* was the American language, *Black Mask's* early stories reflect little awareness of how America was talking as the 1920's began. In 1922 a typical story began: "When Mr. George

Mitchell propped the *News* against the sugar bowl and dug into his matutinal grapefruit, he was unused to interruptions by persons answering classified advertisements; but on this particular morning, the maid casually remarked that there was some one at the door inquiring for a position as chauffeur." And dialogue exchanges like this were still going on:

> "Well," he observed, "it's certainly an odd thing that Sir Cheville Stanbury should come to a violent end immediately after making a will in which he left a pretty considerable sum of money to a young woman on whom his own solicitor was evidently far gone, isn't it?"
>
> "What's to be done?" asked Marston. "Are you going to tell the police?"
>
> "That's precisely what we don't intend! No, no, Sir Marston, what we know or think we'll keep to ourselves for a while! Don't say a word of what we may be thinking to a soul—not even to your mother."

But while Sir Marston worried over what to tell his mother, the real world began to invade *Black Mask*. Prohibition had happened and detective stories that talked about hip flasks, home-made gin and gangsters started appearing alongside the politer tales of the upper classes and English gardens. Gradually, too, *Black Mask* began to attract writers who were trying, sometimes clumsily, not only to deal with home-made problems but to write in the American language and achieve a vernacular style. Out in suburban White Plains, New York, a mild, moustached young man started talking tough:

> Now, when I say I'm an honest man I mean I'm honest to a certain extent. When I deal with an honest man I play him honest and when I deal with a crook I play him—well —I play him at his own game.
>
> You see crooks is my meat. They're simple, almost child-

ish and what makes them easy picking is that they lack a sense of humor.

And now for how I came to have Ed, the Killer, on my trail and gunning for me night and day.

This is Carroll John Daly, early in 1923, a few months after he began selling to *Black Mask*. What Daly is trying to do is come up with a convincing tough private operative who narrates his own adventures. Daly, a former movie projectionist and theater manager, had good intentions, but he suffered from a tin ear. He undoubtedly soaked up too much bad silent movie melodrama as well. Nevertheless, Carroll John Daly invented one of the first of the new breed of private eyes. By June of 1923 he had the character roughed out and named. He was Race Williams and he introduced himself by saying, "I'm what you might call a middleman—just a half-way house between the cops and the crooks . . . I do a little honest shooting once in a while—just in the way of business—but I never bumped off a guy what didn't need it."

Race Williams became one of the most popular pulp characters of the 1920's and '30's. His name, usually in red letters, on a *Black Mask* cover was good for a twenty percent rise in circulation. Race Williams was a tough, straight-shooting, wise-talking, pragmatic urban cowboy. He was cynical, didn't trust anybody. Yet he could be sentimental about a girl in trouble. There were no neat time-table crimes in his world. Mostly he fought against gangsters, crooked politicians and the occasional master criminal Daly couldn't keep from throwing in. Race Williams didn't get along with the police and they were edgy about him, continually warning him not to be so restless in his gunning down of crooks and suspects. "Right and wrong are not written on the statutes for me," explained Race Williams, "nor do I find my code of morals in the essays of long-winded professors. My ethics are my own.

I'm not saying they're good and I'm not admitting they're bad, and what's more I'm not interested in the opinions of others on the subject." He arranged things so his idea of justice triumphed. Most problems can be solved by action. "It's not what you should have done that counts in life," he said. "It's what you do."

The world Race Williams operated in was a nightmare projection of the real world of the '20's and '30's. It was a night world, filled with speakeasies, gambling joints, penthouses, rundown hotels. Hoods kept their hat brims pulled low, packed a .45 in the armpit, drove long black cars. There was no safety. The people Williams was trying to help were continually shot at, kidnapped, tortured. Sometimes he'd have to rescue the same girl several times. Despite the dangers and the unpredictability of things, Race Williams made sure he kept himself in control. "I don't allow the unexpected to happen, if I can prevent it." Like many private detectives to follow, Race Williams was impatient and aggressive. In his nearly thirty years as a detective he kicked down innumerable doors, pushed aside countless bodyguards to get at the boss. And he loved shooting. Shooting with a big .45 automatic:

I squeezed lead—and the show was over. No hero holding his chest and giving a last message to his surviving countrymen. He was dead five times before he hit the floor.

I fired my last shot—not into that generous bulk that had tempted me before, but straight into that red, yawning mouth. We'd see how his digestive system worked. The secret of the bullet-proof body was out; he wore a shirt of steel chain.

He died funny. Yep, I got a laugh out of it; a weird, gurgling sort of a laugh. His mouth seemed to close upon the bullet, as if he tried the taste of it—and his arms still stretched toward me. Then those twitching fingers closed

on empty air. He slipped to his knees, knelt so a moment
—as if in prayer—then pitched forward on his face. Dead?
He was as cold as an old maid's smile.

I just raised my left hand and tightened my finger. He was
leaning over, almost above me, when I let him have it.
Nothing artistic about my shooting then. There wasn't
meant to be. . . . Hulbert Clovelly dropped the knife from
his left hand and clutched at his stomach. He screamed too
—cursed once, and raised his right hand. But he didn't fire
again. I don't know if he had the will or the nerve, or even
the strength to—but I do know he didn't have the chance
to.

Race Williams had the habit of turning to the reader on
occasion and justifying all this killing:

I closed my finger on the trigger and shot the gunman
smack through the side of the head. Hard? Cold-blooded?
Little respect for life? Maybe. But after all, it didn't seem
to me to be the time to argue the point with the would-be
killer.

Of course sometimes Race Williams didn't even have to
shoot. He just showed his guns:

I leaned slightly forward so for a moment he got a flash of
two guns—one under each arm. . . . I said simply, "When
you put Race Williams out of a rat trap like this, you'll
have to put him out in a cloud of smoke."

The word simple appears often in the Carroll John Daly
stories. "In that second I let him have it. Simple? Of
course it was simple." To Race Williams there was no
problem that couldn't be cleared up by simple, active
means. In his adventures, as an advertisement put it, you
found "no long explanations, no discussions of evidence."
Carroll John Daly, working quietly in White Plains, had

invented a fiction type who fitted in with the tempera-
ment of the years between the wars. Not a great talent but
nevertheless a pioneer, Professor Philip Durham sums
him up this way, "Carroll John Daly was a careless writer
and a muddy thinker who created the hard-boiled detective, the prototype for numberless writers to follow."

Fortunately for the future and long-range survival, of
the private eye, Dashiell Hammett occurred at the
same time as Daly. And to Hammett the world was
anything but simple. "I drank a lot in those days," he
later recalled, "partly because I was confused by the
fact that people's feelings and talk and actions didn't
have much to do with one another." The private investigator that Hammett created for *Black Mask* in the
early 1920's was much different than Race Williams, a
more complex and a more subtly handled figure. He
had none of the swagger or the flash of Daly's creation.
He didn't even have a name. He worked as an operative for the Continental Detective Agency in San Francisco and his first person adventures were recounted in
a terse, detached style:

I went up to the Great Western Hotel, dumped my bags,
and went out to look at the city.

It wasn't pretty. Most of its builders had gone in for
gaudiness. Maybe they had been successful at first. But
since then the smelters, whose brick stacks stuck up tall
against a gloomy mountain to the south, had yellow-
smoked everything into a uniform dinginess. The result
was an ugly city of forty thousand people, set in an ugly
notch between two ugly mountains that had been all
dirtied up by mining. Spread over this was a grimy sky
that looked as if it had come out of the smelters' stacks.

The first policeman I saw needed a shave. The second
had a couple of buttons off his shabby uniform. The
third stood in the middle of Personville's main intersec-
tion—Broadway and Union Street—directing traffic with

a cigar in one corner of his mouth. After that I stopped checking them up.

The Continental Op, as Hammett's new detective came to be called, never bragged about his prowess with his fists or guns. He showed you, usually downplaying his ability. After shooting the gun out of a man's hand, for instance, the Op added, "It looks like a great stunt, but it's a thing that happens now and then. A man who is a fair shot (and that is exactly what I am—no more, no less), naturally and automatically shoots pretty close to the spot upon which his eyes are focused." The police didn't look on him as a crazed vigilante. They knew he was a competent professional, a man with several years' experience in the slow patient business of being an investigator, and they cooperated with him on cases.

The first Continental Op story was printed in 1923. Commenting on it in his biography of Hammett, William F. Nolan says: "In that one the Op described himself as 'a busy, middle-aged detective' more interested in solving the crime than in 'feminine beauty.' From the outset, he was anti-women when it came to a case; the Op was all business. When he talked to a woman, 'I discarded the trick stuff—and came out cold-turkey.' He'd been with Continental of San Francisco for 'four or five years' and was an old hand at ducking bullets and reading truth behind lies." Using a restrained vernacular style, utilizing the foggy San Francisco of the 1920's as a setting, Hammett went on to write a series of stories and novels about the Op. Stories with real people, real motives and real murders. Unlike most of his contemporaries in the crime pulps, Hammett had actually been a private detective himself. He had worked several years for the Pinkerton Agency, joining up in his hometown of Baltimore just before World War I. By the middle '20's he quit for good. "I was beginning to sour on being a detective. The excitement was no longer there." He was married now, living in San Francisco and suffering from tuberculosis. Hammett took a job writing copy in the advertising department of a Market Street jeweler. "Hammett wanted to record his unique experiences on paper," explains biographer Nolan, "but fiction was a trade he knew nothing about. So he drank, trying to 'figure things.' Alcohol and lack of sleep undermined his health, and Hammett's lungs gave way again. . . . Ignoring his wife's pleas, Hammett refused hospitalization. They argued. He left his family (by now they had a two-year-old daughter) and rented a cheap hotel room in downtown San Francisco." Hammett made his first sales to Bill Kofoed's *Brief Stories,* a pulp devoted to the short-short. Apparently he aimed next at the *Smart Set*, but missed and hit *Black Mask*. Which resulted in the Continental Op.

The short, heavy-set Continental Op was both sardonic and sentimental. He, too, would shoot a man if he had to and help a girl who needed protecting. He was quiet about it all. When a client becomes overly dramatic in explaining a problem, the Op tells him, "What's the use of getting poetic about it? If you've got an honest job to be done, and want to pay an honest price for it, maybe I'll take it." Despite the fact that he sometimes gets involved with sinister Orientals, family curses and religious cults, Hammett's operative has a realistic conception of detective work. "Ninety-nine percent of detective work is a patient collecting of details." The Op drinks, smokes Fatima cigarettes, but when he is on a case he doesn't get involved with women. When he did feel strongly about a girl, the Op would talk himself and the girl out of it. "Well, good God, sister! I'm only a hired man with a hired man's interest in your troubles."

In 1929, in a *Black Mask* serial, Hammett introduced another private detective. Samuel Spade, who undertook the hunt for the Maltese falcon. Spade was a little less

detached than the Op, a little less restrained. He had been
sleeping with his partner's wife and was not reluctant
about doing the same thing with female clients. Still he
had his code and when his partner is killed, he sets out to
avenge him. Spade didn't get along with the law as well
as the Op. He puts his own interests ahead of theirs. But
he is about as honest as a man can be in the complicated
world he has to function in. Hammett detached himself
a bit more from the Spade adventures by writing in the
third person, but he did give Sam Spade the first name he
himself had abandoned when he began writing. *The Maltese Falcon* introduced a few more of the standard private
eye props, particularly the loyal girl secretary who
guards the outer office.

In 1933, a forty-five-year-old businessman who'd been
hurt by the Depression decided to see if he could write the
kind of private eye stories he'd been enjoying in the pulps.
It took Raymond Chandler five months to turn out his first
story, "Blackmailers Don't Shoot." Joseph Shaw bought it
for *Black Mask* and Chandler gave himself over to writing pulp novelets. Chandler, though educated in England,
was fascinated by the American language. To speak, to
write in a truly American style was important to him and
had been since he was a young man. "I was distinctly not
a clever young man. Nor was I at all a happy young man,"
Chandler said much later. "I had very little money, although there was a great deal of it in my family. I had
grown up in England and all my relatives were either
English or Colonial. And yet I was not English. I had no
feeling of identity with the United States, and yet I re-
sented the kind of ignorant and snobbish criticism of
Americans that was current at the time. During my time
in Paris I had run across a good many Americans, and
most of them seemed to have a lot of bounce and liveli-
ness and to be thoroughly enjoying themselves in situa-
tions where the average Englishman of the same class

would be stuffy or completely bored. But I wasn't one of them. I didn't even speak their language. I was, in effect, a man "without a country." By the early 1930's, a long time after, Chandler had found his country and could speak its language. And he was on his way to finding Philip Marlowe. "Although Philip Marlowe was not introduced by that name until 1939, he had been developing in Chandler's short stories for a half dozen years," points out Philip Durham in an essay on the Black Mask School. "Chandler's original private eye, using the name Mallory, appeared in *Black Mask* in December 1933. From that date through 1939, he performed in twenty short stories, usually as a private eye . . . He used ten different names and was twice nameless, but always a part of the man Marlowe was to become. In experimenting with viewpoint, Chandler used the first person twelve times and the third person eight. Once created Marlowe was always a first person narrator; this technique kept him on the scene, involved in the lives of others."

The first person private eye Chandler was developing, no matter what name he appeared under, always talked in a controlled, vernacular and, at the same time poetic, style:

I went out of the bar without looking back at her, got into my car and drove west on Sunset and down all the way to the Coast Highway. Everywhere along the way gardens were full of withered and blackened leaves and flowers which the hot wind had burned.

But the ocean looked cool and languid and just the same as ever. I drove on almost to Malibu and then parked and went and sat on a big rock that was inside somebody's wire fence. . . . I pulled a string of Bohemian glass imitation pearls out of my pocket and cut the knot at one end and slipped the pearls off one by one.

"To the memory of Mr. Stan Phillips," I said aloud. "Just another four-flusher."

I flipped her pearls out into the water at the floating seagulls.

They made little splashes and the seagulls rose off the water and swooped at the splashes.

Chandler's private eye was a dedicated man, an honest man. He wasn't in it just for the money. Usually he was driven by a stubborn sense of justice. He got along with the police if they were straight. If they were crooked or on the take, he had contempt for them. Most of the stories were set in Southern California, a shabby wonderland Chandler loved to explore and expose. His private eye always operated out of a small rundown office and lived in a small rundown apartment.

Raymond Chandler was fully aware of what he was up to, of what he was doing with the private eye and what his detective stood for. Of his private detective hero he said, "He is a failure and he knows it. He is a failure because he hasn't any money . . . But he is a creature of fantasy. He is in a false position because I put him there . . . Your private detective in real life is usually either an ex-policeman with a lot of hard practical experience and the brains of a turtle or else a shabby little hack who runs around trying to find out where people have moved to." Of his general purpose in writing about private detectives Chandler summed up, "It is not a very fragrant world you live in, and certain writers with tough minds and a cool spirit of detachment can make very interesting and even amusing patterns out of it." As the 1930's ended Chandler turned some of his pulp novelets into a novel called *The Big Sleep*. He sold the book, probably at the suggestion of Joseph Shaw, to publisher Alfred A. Knopf and was soon able to move out of the pulps for good. Hammett had gone through much the same process nearly a decade before.

Raymond Chandler, late in his life, looked back at the hardboiled detective story and *Black Mask* and said, "When a high standard of excellence in a literary field—even a restricted field—has been established, there is a sudden brief flowering of talent in all sorts of writers who will never be heard of again." The '30's, when Chandler himself worked in the pulps, was the decade in which the largest number of talented detective story writers flourished. Chandler was able to progress, to escape from the pulps to hardcovers and to a more comfortable income. He got critical attention, and eventually academic recognition, and he is still known. Most of Chandler's contemporaries, even the gifted ones, did not fare as well. The names Eric Taylor, Paul Cain, W.T. Ballard, John K. Butler, Raoul Whitfield, Roger Torrey, Norbert Davis, J.J. des Ormeaux and H.H. Stinson don't produce much of a shock of recognition now. But although Chandler's stories are almost the sole survivors of the *Black Mask* school of the '30's, he wasn't the only good man doing business then.

One of the pulp stories Chandler remembered reading in the years when he was breaking into the field had the terse title "Red Goose." Referring to it in a letter he wrote, "It must be very good because I have never forgotten it." This mention prompted Chandler to dig out the February, 1934, issue of *Black Mask* and re-read Norbert Davis' story. "Not as good as I thought," the older Chandler felt, "but it's still pretty good." "Red Goose" had been written by Norbert Davis in his college rooming house at Stanford University. He was supposed to be there to get his law degree, but writing became more important. "Bert became so successful," a close friend of his told me, "that he never bothered to take the bar exam." While Shaw was editing *Black Mask,* Davis appeared only occasionally. "Although Shaw said that he could write the best letter of anyone in the business," recalls his friend, "his stuff was too whimsical to fit well into the action pattern." When Shaw put together his anthology, though, he included the Davis story. "Red Goose" begins like this:

> It was a long, high-ceilinged hall, gloomy and silent. The air was musty. Tall, barred windows on one side of the hall let in a little of the bright sunlight where it formed waffle-like patterns on the thick green carpet. There was a polished brass rail, waist-high, running the length of the hall on the side opposite the barred windows.
> Shaley came quietly along the hall. He was whistling softly to himself through his teeth and tapping with his forefinger on the brass rail in time with his steps.... A door at the end of the hall opened, and a wrinkled little man in a gray suit that was too big for him came hurrying out. He carried a framed picture under one arm, and had dusty, rimless glasses on his nose.
> Shaley stepped in front of him and said: "Hello."
> "How do you do," said the little man busily. He didn't look up. He tried to side-step around Shaley.
> Shaley kept in front of him. "My name is Shaley—Ben Shaley."
> "Yes, yes," said the little man absently. He tried to squeeze past.
> Shaley put out one long arm, barring his way.
> "Shaley," he said patiently. "Ben Shaley. You sent for me."
> The little man looked up, blinking through the dusty glasses.
> "Oh!" he said. "Oh! Mr. Shaley. Of course. You're the detective."
> Shaley nodded. "Now you're getting it."

The story draws to a close, after Shaley has hunted down the stolen painting called The Red Goose, a bit more violently:

Shaley got his stiff fingers around the butt of the automatic, pushed the muzzle against Gorjon's side.

At its blasting report the room suddenly cleared in front of Shaley's eyes. Gorjon fell over sidewise, very slowly, and hit the floor and lay there without moving.

Shaley got slowly to his feet, staggering a little. His nose was broken. He could feel the blood running down his face. He started towards Tannerwell and Carter. . . . Carter was amazingly strong and quick. It was like trying to hold a squirming ball of soft rubber. He got one leg loose, kicked Shaley in the face. He hit Shaley's nose, and Shaley writhed on the floor, swearing thickly, losing his grip on Carter's legs.

Carter bounced to his feet instantly. He ran down the hall towards the stairs.

"Carter!"

It was Marjorie Smith. She was standing in the doorway and she had the .45 automatic . . . Carter whirled around like a dancer and jumped sidewise crouching. Marjorie Smith shot him.

Marjorie Smith shot him again, deliberately, in the back. Carter collapsed weakly and slid down the stairs, bumping soddenly on each step. . . .

Davis, who was not always this violent, specialized in tough, fast and often whimsical private eye stories. This is what Raymond Chandler was attempting in his own stories and is one of the reasons he was fond of Norbert Davis' work. Davis wrote a great quantity of pulp material in the '30's and '40's, appearing eventually in most of the pulp detective magazines as well as *Argosy*. He also had some luck in slicks like *The Saturday Evening Post* before his early death in 1949. The career of Norbert Davis is representative of those of the writers mentioned above. Promising men who never gained very much notice beyond the pages of *Black Mask* and the other detective pulps.

Black Mask did not get any real competition in the tough detective field until the 1930s. In the '20's *Clues, Detective Fiction Weekly* and *Detective Story* gave little space to the kind of story Joseph Shaw was championing. "It was often said, in that period," Shaw later wrote of his authors, "that their product, in its best examples, was several years ahead of its time. These writers were blazing new paths." After the Depression had hit, the paths were clear enough to follow. Of the minor impersonators, the most interesting was Fiction House's *Black Aces*. This short-lived pulp magazine found it easier to imitate the *Black Mask* format than its content. Starting from the cover, *Black Aces* tried to look as much like *Black Mask* as it could. Even the editorial page was signed in an imitation of Shaw's signature. Fiction House neglected to run many stories that could match those in *Black Mask,* though they did get a few of Shaw's contributors to write for them.

The strongest competitor was *Dime Detective*. Inaugurated in 1932 as part of Popular Publication's low-price line, the magazine was at first a disparate blend of private eye stories and old dark house melodramas. It was advertised then as a magazine of "mystery . . . thrills . . . terror" and for every tough and realistic story there were two with titles like "The Screeching Skull" and "The Green Ghoul." By the mid 1930's, under the editorship of Kenneth S. White, *Dime Detective* was almost completely given over to the kind of story Shaw had pioneered. The terror stories moved into Popular's *Dime Mystery,* which we'll look at it in a later chapter. "Ken White had tried to copy *Black Mask* with *Dime,*" W.T. Ballard told me, "but for some reason it never quite came off. I had known Ken for many years and used to kid him about being jealous of Shaw, which he was." After Joseph Shaw left *Black Mask* in 1936, the editorship was given to Fanny Ellsworth, a lady who had been editing *Ranch Romances.*

Quite a few of the veteran contributors switched to *Dime Detective*. Most notable was Raymond Chandler, who did the last of his pulp writing for the magazine. In the early '40's *Black Mask* itself was sold to Popular and Kenneth White got to edit not only the imitation but the real thing as well. White featured the regulars like Ballard, Norbert Davis and Roger Torrey in both magazines and added some new people. D.L. Champion gave up the Phantom Detective and began to look prolific under his own name. He did several series of whimsical detective stories for White. Merle Constiner, who now does very distinctive Western novels, contributed two excellent groups of stories to the magazines. One series dealt with an amiable charlatan of a detective named The Dean and the other with an outspoken private detective, Luther McGavock, who worked the rural South.

Eventually almost all the detective pulps were featuring private eye stories. The Munsey Company's *Detective Fiction Weekly,* which enjoyed a great number of different editors, used considerable hardboiled material in the '30's. Street & Smith also offered tough, though slightly tamer, stories in *Crimebusters, Clues* (taken over from Clayton) and *Mystery.* The more sedate *Detective Story* even gave some room to private detectives. Particularly in its later years under the editorship of Daisy Bacon, who had a fondness for the work of the Shaw alumni.

No survey of the private eye pulps would be complete without a mention of perhaps the most memorable dick of them all—Dan Turner, Hollywood detective. S.J. Perelman was fascinated by him, calling Dan Turner "the apotheosis of all private eyes. Out of Ma Barker by Dashiell Hammett's Sam Spade." Dan Turner began his career in the middle 1930's in *Spicy Detective,* and was the creation of Robert Leslie Bellem. In the early 1940's the publishers yielded to what one editor recalls as "pressure from somewhere" and dropped the *Spicy* from the title.

Dan Turner then became the star of *Hollywood Detective* magazine. Bellem wrote not only the Dan Turner stories, but under an assortment of pennames, the entire magazine. He always used his real name when writing of Dan Turner. The first person style Bellem devised for these detective adventures of Dan Turner is so colloquial, flippant, tough and high-speed that Turner comes across as the best parody private eye ever done. A typical caper opens:

> I growled: "Hey, what the hell—!" and raised my bedroom window, peered out into the foggy midnight. Whereupon a tall and much too handsome bozo on the fire escape fetched me a vicious clout over the thatch with a set of brass knuckles.

Dan Turner is a blownup version of Race Williams and an anticipation of Spillane's Mike Hammer. He is tough with men:

> I ducked another punch and caught him a loping right on the bridge work.

> My fist caught him in the jaw. He let me have his knee in the groin. . . . Somehow the gun went off again. A slug went tearing through the guy's guts. Maybe I killed him; maybe he killed himself. I didn't know—and I didn't give a damn.

But Dan Turner is even tougher with women:

> I said: "Baby, this is going to hurt a little!" Then I pasted her across the face with the flat of my hand.

> A sleepy chink maid in pajamas answered my ring. She was a cute little slant-eyed number. I said, "Is Mr. Pulznak home?" She shook her head. "Him up on location in Fresno. Been gone two week." I said, "Thanks. I'll have a gander for myself." I pushed past her. She started to yip . . .

"Shut up!" I growled. She kept on trying to make noise. So I popped her on the button. She dropped.

If there's anything I dislike, it's having some misguided skirt probing my sacro-iliac with a rodney. . . . So I did something about the situation. I pivoted on my heel, used my left elbow as a bludgeon. That whopped the gun aside. Simultaneously I grabbed for it, got it, shoved it in my pocket. Then I fastened the clutch on this homicidal female, yanked her inside the room, and kicked the door closed.

Among Dan Turner's other mannerisms is a fondness for smoking, always described as "I set fire to a gasper." He tended to hear the sound of gun shots in a particular way:

From the window behind me a roscoe sneezed: "Ka-Chow!"

My borrowed cannon sneezed: "Ka-Chow!"

From the doorway a roscoe said "Kachow!" and a slug creased my noggin.

Like his private detective, Robert Leslie Bellem lived and worked in the Hollywood area. After *Hollywood Detective,* like the rest of the private eye pulps, folded in the early 1950's Bellem turned to writing movies and television scripts. One of the shows he worked on was Dick Tracy.

CHAPTER NINE

COWBOYS

Action, action, action is the thing. So long as you keep your hero jumping through fiery hoops on every page you're all right. The basic formula I use is simple: good man turns bad, bad man turns good. Naturally, there is considerable variation on this theme. . . . There has to be a woman, but not much of a one. A good horse is much more important.
—*Max Brand*

In 1919, Street & Smith overhauled another of their elderly periodicals and the *New Buffalo Bill Weekly* became *Western Story Magazine*, a bi-weekly. Frank Blackwell, who'd been on hand when *Nick Carter* turned into *Detective Story*, was made editor of this latest transmutation. The first issue of *Western Story* in pulp format was dated September 5, 1919, and contained stories by such authors as Bertrand W. Sinclair, of Edinburgh, Scotland, and William McLeod Raine, who hailed originally from London.

Within a year Western Story hit a circulation of three hundred thousand per issue and it was made into a weekly, which it stayed for the next quarter century. Like all successful pulps *Western Story* inspired imitations. By the late 1920's the pulp magazines devoted exclusively to cowboy fiction were numerous. These included *West* and *Frontier*, published by Doubleday; *Cowboy Stories, Ace-High, Ranch Romances* and *Western Adventures* from the Clayton house; *Triple-X Western*, published by Fawcett, who were moving up in sophistication from *Capt. Billy's Whiz-Bang; Western Trails, Golden West, Riders Of The Range* and *Western Outlaws*, all from ex-Clayton editor Harold Hersey; *Lariat* and *North-West Stories*, both published by Fiction House, the outfit started by Jack Glenister, who had been business manager for the *Smart Set-Black Mask* group. *North-West* was actually, as its title suggests, only half Western. "The world's only all Western and Northern story magazine," is how it described itself. "Vigorous, tingling epics of the great *Snow* FRONTIER and the IMMORTAL WEST! Two thin dimes buy hours of joyous adventure."

When the 1930's arrived two thin dimes were considered a high price for a magazine and even cheaper westerns began to appear on the stands. Ned Pines and his inventive editorial director, Leo Margulies, filled the Depression market with titles: *Thrilling Western, Thrilling Ranch Stories, Popular Western, Texas Rangers,* etc. All at ten cents a copy. While Pines and Margulies were applying the word thrilling to various pulp types, Popular Publications was having fun with the word dime. Their *Dime Western* is said to be one of the two pulps subscribed to by Franklin Delano Roosevelt. A *Nickel Western* also appeared in 1932, but it was too slim to survive. Street & Smith had by now gotten around to issuing more western pulps of its own. They'd added *Far West, Wild West Weekly* and *Pete Rice Magazine.* Everything in the weekly, which was another revitalized old fiction weekly started early in the century, was written in a sort of interchangeable house prose. The magazine was, especially in the 1930's, a hotbed of series characters. Particularly when it came to cowboys nicknamed Kid. *Wild West Weekly* offered its readers the Silver Kid, the Oklahoma Kid, the Whistlin' Kid, the Montana Kid and Kid Wolf. The *Pete Rice Magazine* was built around a cowboy with a coterie of distinctive sidekicks. Street & Smith hoped he'd do as well as Doc Savage and his coterie of distinctive sidekicks, but he didn't.

The '30's also saw the appearance of such assorted cowboy titles as *Crack Shot, Ace Western, Quick-Trigger, Double-Action, Six-Gun, Big-Book Western* and *New Western.* Frank Armer, whose favorite word was spicy, was right in there with *Spicy Western.* Even the Lone Ranger, who was selling a lot of bread on the radio at the time, appeared in a short-lived pulp magazine of his own. This, too, was published by Frank Armer, who apparently had enough restraint not to call it *Spicy Lone Ranger.*

The writers who rode the pulp range were legion. Most of them are forgotten, their reputations in no better shape today than the yellow and crumbling pulp paper on which their stories appeared. Among them were James B. Hendryx, who did as many Northerns as he did Westerns; Harry Sinclair Drago, who was also Bliss Lomax and Will Ermine; Henry Herbert Knibbs, a Canadian-born poet who made a living with pulp westerns and specialized in horse stories; Jackson Gregory, a native of California, who was first a high school principal and then, after World War I, a writer; Foster-Harris, who was actually William Foster Harris with no hyphen and who explained his basic story formula as $1+1=2$; Borden Chase, who, according to Frank Gruber, thought up his penname while watching a Borden truck drive by the Chase Manhattan Bank; J.J. des Ormeaux, who also wrote for *Black*

Mask. A novelet of his in *Dime Western* opens with one of the most evocative lines ever: "On the spot where Hollywood would some day grow two vaqueros were crushing a priest to death with his own wine-press."

Clarence E. Mulford wrote for the pulps, too. Illinois-born, Mulford started writing while holding down a civil service job in New York. In the early years of the century he sold a series of cowboy stories to a travel monthly called *Outing Magazine.* The stories dealt with the men of the Bar 20 Ranch and their trail boss, Hopalong Cassidy. Although when he first wrote of the West, Mulford had never seen it, his Bar 20 tales are not romantic and exaggerated but played-down and realistic. He once explained, "The first books were published from data, but later I traveled throughout the West. . . . I have an extensive library of Western Americana, and have thrown away three times as many books as I retained. My card file of Western data, more than 17,000 cards, covers every activity of the West." The book and pulp Hopalong Cassidy was not at all like the William Boyd movie character. Mulford's Cassidy was a rough, tobacco-chewing redhead with nothing fancy about him. In a way, Mulford personifies two of the basic kinds of pulp Western writer. The man who fantasizes at a distance about the cowboy life and the man who writes out of first-hand knowledge of the West. Mulford was able to fuse imagination with experience and research. Many other writers would be able to get by on only one part of that trinity. It didn't seem to matter. The cowboy magazines were always the best selling of the pulps and they used up an enormous amount of material, from honest and authentic to false and unreal.

Frederick Schiller Faust stood six feet three inches and weighed 220 pounds. He wanted to be a poet. But to make a living, after graduating from the University of California at Berkeley, he turned to pulp writing. A friend

suggested that Frederick Schiller Faust wasn't the right
kind of name for a writer of adventure and invented Max
Brand for him to use. Faust, anxious to reserve his real
name for his serious work, gladly adopted the new penname. He and another beginning writer, John Schoolcraft, shared a room in New York City during the World
War I years. "We were extremely hard up," Schoolcraft
recalled. "We found a place which supplied a huge plate
of beans for fifteen cents—and as a consequence ate beans
three times a day . . . There was no coal. Water spilled on
the floor of our room, froze, and stayed frozen for weeks.
One morning the thermometer stood at eight below zero,
and a wind was coming out of the North as cold as the
heart of Frank A. Munsey." It was Munsey's warm-
hearted editor, Robert H. Davis, who began to buy Faust's
stories. "Davis handed his young protege a copy of Grey's
Riders Of The Purple Sage, suggesting that Faust try his
hand in the lucrative Western field," recounts William F.
Nolan in his study of Max Brand. "Faust responded with
an 85,000 word saga (starring a god-like youngster, 'Whistling Dan' Barry) which he called 'The Untamed.' When
the story appeared as a six-parter in *All-Story* in 1918 it
proved a huge success with readers." Editor Bob Davis,
while noted for his frequent kindnesses to many young
and struggling writers, was not acting completely from
altruistic motives in the case of Faust. Zane Grey's purple
prose horse epics had done wonders for the circulation of
the Munsey pulps when they'd been serialized there. No
doubt, now that Grey was on the hardcover bestseller
lists, Davis was looking for new authors who could repeat
Grey's successes and not ask his prices.

Faust had grown up in the West, working since his
teens on the farms and ranches of California's San Joa-
quin Valley. Yet he never admitted his Westerns had anything to do with real life and referred to his cowboy stories as "the old melodramatic junk." Max Brand had

begun turning out this junk in quantity just before Street
& Smith's *Western Story Magazine* was born. He sold his
first story to Frank Blackwell in 1920 and it appeared in
the November, 1920, issue. Faust went on to sell over
three hundred stories, novelets and serials to that single
market. Serial installments running over several issues
stretch Brand's total number of appearances in *Western
Story* to 834. Besides being Max Brand for Blackwell,
Faust was also George Owen Baxter, David Manning and
Evan Evans, among others. "From *Western Story Magazine* alone," reports William F. Nolan, "Faust earned
nearly a million dollars, contributing thirteen million
words in thirteen years to that weekly publication under
eleven pennames. *Destry Rides Again* was written during
this period, a book which was to sell more than a million
copies and be made into several films."

Under his multitude of names, Faust turned out all
sorts of cowboy writing. He could be lyrical:

> Then, looking down the starlit hollow, he saw the horse-
> man sweep across it like the shadow of a low-swooping
> hawk. Up the hillside came the stranger, into the circle of
> the fire, and then dropped to the ground, lightly, as one
> who has not ridden a mile, though the salty incrustations
> on the hide of the black mare proved that the day had been
> a long and weary one for her. But though she was tired, her
> eyes were as bright and her head as high as that of her
> handsome young master.

Or tough:

> I didn't try to aim, either. I just threw the gun out of half-
> arm distance, and fired at the blur of Bert as the form of
> him jumped into line with my vision. He was around, too,
> and fully facing me. Perhaps he had lost a part of a second
> in making so full a turn. At any rate, he only fired his
> weapon into the ground, a spasmodic, natural contraction

of the hand. For my bullet had gone home. I heard the spat
of it against his face like the clapping of hands together.
He threw a forearm across his forehead, covering the
wound, and dropped straight forward. His body hit with a
loose, jostling sound, then he lay still.

Even flat:

> Then, eager with haste but stealthy with fear of what
> might lie before him, Litton stole rapidly forward through
> the trees, feeling with his hands outstretched, and putting
> his feet down toes first.

As of 1970, over two hundred different Faust books, most
of them pulp originals, have been printed and more are
coming. These include *Singing Guns, Fightin' Fool, The
Longhorn Fued, Silvertip* and *Calling Dr. Kildare.*

In the 1930's Faust lived in Italy. "He lived like a Re-
naissance prince with his wife and family in the hills
above Florence," says Nolan. "His villa boasted one of the
largest private tennis courts in Italy. Here he indulged
himself in golf, riding, swimming, chess, bridge, as-
tronomy, gardening and cooking. . . . Each morning at the
villa, Faust would carefully craft his scraps of verse, then
—after lunch—retire to his study to rap out his daily
10,000 words of pulp melodrama." In order to make those
daily transitions from poetry to prose, Faust convinced
himself he had to drink. He drank sherry or Irish whisky
in the morning, beer and wine in the afternoon, cocktails
before dinner, wine with dinner and a night-cap later.
His letters to friends fluctuate between declarations that
"the booze is now well in hand" to admissions that "I now
find I can only write when I am drinking." In the late '30's,
Faust went to Hollywood and also wrote for slicks like
Collier's. When the war started he got himself accredited
as a war correspondent for *Harper's.* He wrote to his wife

from Italy, "I can't help hoping I shall come out of this a better man. I have always wished I could turn a corner, climb a higher stair." He was killed in May of 1944 while charging a German artillery position in the Italian hills. He had gone up with the young soldiers. He was fifty-two, the oldest correspondent at the front lines.

W.C. Tuttle's full name was Wilbur Coleman Tuttle and perhaps this contributed to his developing a sense of humor. In the years between the two World Wars he was the pulp field's predominant writer of the funny cowboy yarn and of the vernacular tall tale. A real Westerner, Tuttle was born in the early 1880's on a ranch in Glendive, Montana. "I was born in the winter of the big snows," Tuttle said. "My father was a buffalo hunter at the time. . . . My education consisted of several years in a little cow-town school, where a diploma consisted of calluses on the knees, due to outgrowing the benches. My last year was spent sitting sideways in the seat, and a lot of folks thought I was over educated." Tuttle drifted considerably in his early years, working as cowpuncher, sheepherder, miner. "The career of a perfectly good cowboy was spoiled when I went to Portland, Oregon, to sell harness and saddles," he recalled. "Lasted one year. Quit that in favor of becoming assistant train master, but quit that in favor of going fishing through the ice." Tuttle then settled down and became an editorial cartoonist for a Spokane newspaper and stayed with it for ten years. While doing newspaper work he decided he could write funnier stories than he was reading in the pulps. He wrote one and sent it to Arthur Sullivant Hoffman at *Adventure.* The story sold. Tuttle was paid twenty-five dollars and decided to get married.

Eventually he wrote for most of the major Western pulps, as well as for *Adventure, Argosy, Short Stories* and *Bluebook.* W.C. Tuttle's out-and-out comedy stories usually take place in disreputable little towns with names like Bearpaw, Salt Rock, Plenty Stone Creek and Scorpion Bend. These stories and novelets are rich with characters named Magpie Simpkins, Tombstone Todd, Hair Oil Heppner, Muley Bowles, Hootie McClung and Warhoop Wilson. The characters, both cowboys and Indians, in these tales are about as honest and presentable as those in W.C. Fields' Western, *My Little Chickadee*. Tuttle tended to write his funny stuff in this style:

Me and Dirty Shirt Jones are settin' on the hitch rack in front of Buck Masterson's saloon one mornin', like a couple old buzzards, lookin' for something to happen. Dirty Shirt ain't very big, but he's got a man size capacity for anythin' you might mention. His left eye is his predominatin' feature, bein' as it ain't noways fixed like a regular eye, but kinda darts hither and yon.

I tries to talk Skeeter out of it, but he's too mad to listen to me. So over that fence he goes and makes a run at that bull-ostrich. Later on, while readin' up on the subject, I find that it just ain't done by the best ostrich handlers.

Tuttle was not always in this mood, but even in his straighter Western stories and novels he usually stuck with alliterative nicknames and dropped letters. To Tuttle the way names were used and the style of expression were important.

Goliath turned to the dark, heavy-jawed cowpuncher sitting on the edge of a bunk, and his easy-going manner suddenly became formally polite. "Would you like to join us for a hand or two of draw, Stark?"

The use of the last name instead of the first, or the more usual nickname, was as indicative as the change from slangy badinage to the more stilted correct English. Any cowman, hearing, would have said immediately that here was either a late-comer, a comparative stranger to the outfit, or else one whom the speaker was not on pleasant terms with.

Tuttle wrote about several cowboy heroes, but probably his best known and most successful books were the relatively straight adventure Westerns he wrote about a range detective with the non-heroic name of Hashknife Hartley. Hashknife first appeared in *Adventure* in 1920, accompanied by a sidekick known as Sleepy Stevens. The team looked like this:

> Hashknife was several inches over six feet in height, with a long, serious face, wide mouth and calculating gray eyes. His raiment was typical of the range country, from battered sombrero to high-heeled boots. At his right sat a man whose dress was identical to his own; a broad-shouldered cowboy, of medium height who wore his sombrero tilted at a rakish angle and gazed with wide blue eyes at nothing in particular; his lips were puckered in an unmusical, low-pitched whistle.

As to their basic philosophy:

> And that was the greatest inducement—the other side of the hill. They always wanted to see the other side of the hill; and when they had seen it there were more hills to lure them on. They were a restless breed, these two; confirmed fatalists, intensely human.
>
> A job meant nothing to them. Fate had thrown them together on the old Hashknife ranch, which had given George Hartley his nickname. Son of a range minister, one of a big family of children, "Hashknife" Hartley had struck out early in life for himself, living the only life he knew—the life of a cowboy.
>
> With but little schooling he had educated himself in his own way, fighting, dreaming, grinning his way along.

Born with an inquisitive mind, he had developed an un-canny ability to puzzle things out for himself.

And when he had become a bunkie of Dave Stevens, otherwise known as "Sleepy," the wide ranges called so strongly that they packed their bed-rolls and rode away from their steady jobs to become wanderers of the range-land.

They laughed at life and death. And they knew death. Death had ridden knee-to-knee with them many times, and they had laughed in his face. They had seen him through the smoke of a forty-five in saloons, gambling houses; they had heard his voice in the open ranges, speak-ing from hidden places.

But always they had laughed at him and rode on toward the next hill.

Hashknife and Sleepy stayed in business for over thirty years.

Walt Coburn was another Montana man who tried the cowboy story. He took his first crack in 1922, using the more formal name Walter J. Coburn. "After two years of rejection slips I sold around nine hundred novelets to thirty-seven different magazines," Coburn has said. "I had the cover and feature story in each magazine over those years." In the last days of the Western pulps Coburn even had a magazine named after him. About his meth-ods of working Coburn said, "I do little research. I knew the early cow country about which I write, cowmen, cow punchers, sheepmen, Indians, *et al,* before the barbed wire fenced the free range." He added, "I have never read another Western author's work in my lifetime of writ-ing."

William MacLeod Raine was born in London in 1871 and he was writing pulp Western stories before there were Western pulps. He came to the United States in the early 1880's and eventually settled in Colorado. The first piece of fiction he sold was a 12,000-word swashbuckler full of swordsmen and not cowmen. He sold it to *Argosy*. "I have never seen a piece of literature that had for me the personal significance of that yarn when I actually read it on the printed page," Raine said some twenty years after the fact. "I went over it a dozen times and always discovered unexpected merits. Little did Denver suspect that the sallow youth walking down Sixteenth Street was a Great Author." Raine soon turned to producing Western stories as well, and selling them to the existing general fiction pulps. As we've noted, he was in the first issue of the first Western pulp. He was still at it in the 1930's and by then had produced such novels as *Beyond The Rio Grande* and *Gunsight Pass*.

One of the more gifted of the writers who worked in the pulps was Ernest Haycox, who also came from out of the West. Born in Portland, he grew up working on ranches and in logging camps. He served with the National Guard on the Mexican border in 1916 and in France with the AEF during World War I. He began freelancing in even humbler circumstances than Max Brand, living and working in an abandoned chicken house. Haycox said he papered three walls of the place with rejection slips before his work began to sell. He moved to New York and better quarters in the '20's, stayed long enough to establish himself and get married. Then he came back to the West and remained there until his death in 1950.

His stories were action stories, filled with gun fights, chases and showdowns. But many of his heroes, despite their pulp Western names, are complex, patient, introspective men. Haycox wrote of violence in a quirky, sometimes sensual way, and his pulp stories must be among the few to show a man becoming really attracted to, and often aroused by, a woman.

Directly afterward the door opened, and she stood slim and smiling against the daylight flooding her room. At once pulled out of his thinking, Dan Smith let his attention remain on her. It wasn't often a man saw a woman alive and eager like that, a woman wrapped up as she seemed to be in the dapper figure waiting at the door.

When the hero of this story, *The Hour Of Fury*, first speaks to this girl he says, "Most of the grief in this world comes from what people do to each other. But it isn't worth tears. Nothing's worth tears." Later, in a final confrontation with the villain, Smith tells him, "Power is a false light in the far desert." Not many other pulp cowboys were talking, or thinking, like that in those days.

Haycox was as intense about violence, and as lyric, as he was about a restless yearning for the heroine. Here is his hero, Frank Peace, about to be shot at:

> Silence flowed around him. . . . Somewhere along the hall a board squeaked and small as that sound was, it was like a dynamite explosion to Frank Peace. He wheeled in his tracks, ramming his fist into his coat pocket to grip the revolver he carried there. A doorway across the hall swung quietly back on its hinges. He saw somebody moving in the depths of that room's blackness and immediately he swayed aside. At the same moment a round bloom of ragged light burst through the doorway. The breath of the bullet licked across his face and the whole building swelled and shook with the detonation. The slug struck into the wall behind Peace with a small, snoring report.
>
> Peace dropped to the floor, his long, loose body flattened against the boards; the marksman across the way let out a windy sigh and began to rake the room with rapid, plunging fire.

Eventually Haycox graduated out of the pulps and into the slicks. One of his short stories was made into the movie *Stagecoach*, which established John Wayne as a star.

Down the ladder somewhere from the pulps that featured such men as Haycox and Brand and Tuttle were the Thrilling publications, masterminded by Leo Margulies. These cowboy pulps most often offered a ground-out blend of quickie "B" movie thrills and penny dreadful prose. Most of Margulies' big name Western writers were as fictitious as his cowboys. For instance, Jackson Cole who flourished in the 1930's. Jackson Cole was a penname, possibly inspired by the Wyoming town of Jackson Hole. The main works attributed to Cole were the monthly novels about crack Texas Ranger Jim Hatfield, which ran in *Texas Rangers* magazine. The two writers who did most of the forty-five thousand-word novels about Hatfield were Tom Curry and A. Leslie. They took turns at it. Curry remembers doing "about every other issue" from the start of the magazine in 1936 to 1950. Leslie, who is still doing Western paperbacks as Bradford Scott, had a lusher style than Curry. He also came up with the format, such as it was, for the Texas Ranger novels. "He was, I think, inspired by the Lone Ranger," says Curry of Leslie. "He called Hatfield the Lone Wolf and instead of Silver, his horse was called Goldie."

It is not difficult to tell Leslie's Jackson Cole work from that of Curry and others. The Leslie style has a peculiar ring all its own. Here, for example is the opening of a 1936 *Thrilling Western* novel he signed his own name to:

Night! With the golden stars of Nevada hanging in clusters above the mountain tops. The blue-black bowl of the sky was brimful of the moon's white fire, which a wailing wind stirred 'round and 'round until it spilled over the edges and poured a silver torrent down upon the world.

The howl of a coyote drifted from a low ledge and simmered about in the purple sage as if a score of beasts were plainting. Somewhere a night bird called with monotonous grief. The wind crooned to itself as it walked its blue way over the prarie.

At a penny a word, Leslie's already earned himself a dollar just setting the stage. Here is an equally lovely Texas Ranger novel start:

> The cyclopean eye of the Texas night—a wan, waning moon—spread a leprous light over the saw-toothed battlements of the grim Guadalupes. The eerie lunail glow extended out over the vast corrugated reaches of the Cerro Diablo, striving vainly to penetrate the chinks in their massive sides. Chola cacti spread their weirdly gnarled and twisted spiny arms, [etc.]

This time Leslie makes a $1.58 before anybody rides into view.

Series characters were plentiful in the Thrilling magazines, as we saw in the chapter on masked avengers. There was the Masked Rider, mentioned earlier, and even Zorro himself appeared in one of the Margulies Westerns during Johnston McCulley's declining years. Another well-known cowboy regular was the Rio Kid. The Rio Kid, who appeared in the magazine of that name, was the creation of Tom Curry. The Kid was "a man who had been a scout for General George A. Custer against the great cavalry of Jeb Stuart, Confederate leader. Now that the Civil War was over Bob Pryor, known along the Border where his home had been as the Rio Kid, had not lost the cunning learned during his scouting days in the army." Curry estimates he did perhaps forty pulp novels about Bob Pryor and his fighting pards. He was paid a half-cent a word, roughly $250 per novel. The Thrilling combine bought all rights but Curry obtained Margulies' verbal okay to sell the hardcover book rights. Provided, however, he did not use the name Rio Kid. So Curry went over his manuscripts and changed each mention of the Kid and sold the novels to an outfit called Arcadia House. They issued the stories as the adventures of Captain Mesquite. The Pines magazines survived into the 1950's with their Western titles and their *Ranch Romances,* a late assimilation, was still coming out quarterly in the 1960's. Leo Margulies has a company of his own now, the chief publication of which is *Mike Shayne's Mystery Magazine.* When I talked to him a few months ago in his New York City office he gave me a free copy of his newest, *Zane Grey's Magazine.* A Western.

CHAPTER TEN

TARZAN AND THE BARBARIANS

I had good reason for thinking I could sell what I wrote. I had gone thoroughly through some of the all-fiction magazines, and made up my mind that if people were paid for writing rot such as I read I could write just as rotten.

—*Edgar Rice Burroughs*

THE first pulp writing Edgar Rice Burroughs got involved with was the copy for those little ads in the back pages. In his middle thirties, after dropping out of or failing at prep school, the U.S. Cavalry, the stationery business, mining, the auto battery industry, accounting and the mail-order utensil business, Burroughs took a job buying advertising space for a quack alcoholism cure. Though he didn't hold this job for long either, it got him interested in the pulp magazines. After reading the fiction in *Argosy, Blue Book* and *All-Story,* Burroughs decided that here perhaps was something he might not fail at.

In 1911, he wrote and sold a science fiction novel to Munsey's *All-Story*. The novel was printed as "Under The Moons of Mars" and Burroughs had originally signed the penname Normal Bean to it, indicating his sense of humor had not yet fully flowered. This story of swordplay, red princesses and green giants introduced Burroughs' first series hero, John Carter of Mars. The next year he invented Tarzan.

Tarzan of the Apes, for which Burroughs was paid seven hundred dollars, appeared in the October, 1912 issue of *All-Story*. The novel was billed on the cover as a Romance of the Jungle and Burroughs used his real name this time. In his maiden jungle romance Burroughs proved he had indeed studied the pulps, as well as much of the popular fiction of the past several decades. The first Tarzan story is full of borrowings, everything from Kipling's Jungle Books to Frank R. Stockton's *The Casting Away of Mrs. Lecks and Mrs. Aleshine*. One of Burroughs' gifts was an ability to make the most intricate patchworks look like all his own work and read like a smooth flowing narrative. He was to spend the next thirty years mixing bits of Rudyard Kipling, Talbot Mundy, H. Rider Haggard, Jack London, Zane Grey and his own sideshow imagination and calling the results adventure novels. He became a millionaire doing it. In 1912 no one complained about Tarzan being derivative.

According to Sam Moskowitz, in his history of the Munsey pulps, "From the instant the story was distributed, the letters came like a torrent. The readers were delighted . . . They pleaded, demanded, and threatened dire consequences if a sequel was not written . . . [*All-Story*] had discovered dozens of famed authors before and would develop and discover scores

more, but none had arroused reader interest of such en-
thusiastic proportions as Edgar Rice Burroughs."

A success at something at last, Burroughs continued to
write for the pulps throughout the World War I period
and the 1920's. He tried historical novels and Westerns,
returning frequently to John Carter and Tarzan. His
main objectives were those of most freelance writers, getting more assignments and higher word rates.

The second jungle novel, "The Return of Tarzan," was
serialized in Street & Smith's *New Story Magazine* in
1913. In 1914 Tarzan was back with Munsey for "The
Beasts of Tarzan." Thereafter Tarzan swung from magazine to magazine, turning up in *Blue Book* and *Argosy,* as
well as in slicks like *Liberty* and *Redbook.* In 1939 a Tarzan story showed up in the Margulies pulp *Thrilling Adventures.* By this time Burroughs had been the ape man's
biographer for nearly thirty years and must have become
quite weary of loincloths and lost cities. A former Munsey
editor told me that one of his regular jobs in the 1930's
was rewriting Burroughs' manuscripts and getting them
into printable form.

When he commenced the Tarzan novels, Burroughs
knew almost nothing about Africa, and absolutely nothing about primitive man. And though he had spent part
of his life in the West and outdoors, he based Tarzan not
on what he knew first hand but on what he imagined and
what he had read in other romances. This was his great
good fortune, since it enabled him to create a much more
acceptable and appealing jungle man. At the end of *Tarzan of the Apes,* when Tarzan gives up Jane and tells her
his mother was an ape, not a reader believes him. The one
thing he isn't is an ape. Tarzan proves to the reader, and
it is a very satisfying thing to have proved, that there is
something innate in man that makes him come up smell-
ing like a gentleman no matter where you throw him. For
all his dancing with the great apes and sniffing at the

wind, Tarzan is really a nice middle-class white man who just happened to be raised in the jungle. His environment didn't overwhelm him and his true nobility triumphed. This notion is strongly appealing to adolescent boys, who spend considerable time trying not to let their own environment get the best of them. Edgar Rice Burroughs' faith in the eventual triumph of the middle-class mercantile ethic, mixed with his love of derring-do and endangered princesses, helped make Tarzan one of the most successful characters ever to appear on pulpwood paper.

This success of Tarzan's did not go unnoticed and thinking up a workable imitation of the jungle lord was one of the minor preoccupations of the pulp houses from 1912 on. In the '30's, when Johnny Weismuller was using the talkies, sparingly, to earn an even wider popularity for the character, there was a wave of Tarzan imitations. Pulp author Otis Adelbert Kline, whose specialty was imitating Burroughs, tried several Tarzan impersonations during this period, including a serial in *Weird Tales* about a boy raised by tigers in Burma.

Blue Book, not content with Tarzan himself, tried others of the breed. In the middle 1930's they tried Kioga. Kioga, whose adventures were credited to William Chester, was marooned in the Arctic and raised "to a splendid manhood" by a lost tribe of Indians. The frozen wilds are technically not the jungle, but Kioga behaved and dressed close enough to the Tarzan style to be listed among the jungle men. His similarity to Tarzan was enhanced by the fact that in *Blue Book* the estimable Herbert Morton Stoops illustrated both characters' adventures.

The jungle story, with or without ape man, was always a salable commodity. All the general adventure pulps mentioned in an earlier chapter gave space to daring expeditions into dense jungles. The African jungles were the most frequented, but South America, Borneo, New Guinea and anyplace else the foliage was thick also served as settings for pulp adventures. Like most popular genres, the jungle tale eventually inspired magazines devoted exclusively to it. Early in the Depression the faltering W.M. Clayton issued *Jungle Stories* and at about the same time Harold Hersey put together *Thrills of the Jungle.* Neither of these titles thrived.

Few pulps seem to have been devoted exclusively to one jungle character. Though according to Burroughs biographer Richard A. Lupoff *"Ka-Zar* by 'Bob Byrd' was featured in a magazine bearing his name, for several issues starting in 1937. Ka-Zar ... was raised by lions." About the only long-running pulp imitator of Tarzan was a blond jungle man named Ki-Gor. He managed to stay in operation from 1939 until the middle 1950's in *Jungle Stories,* a quarterly published by Fiction House. This is not the same magazine Clayton had tried, nor, for that matter, is it exactly the same Fiction House. The pulp outfit bearing this name had sunk in the early '30's and then been revived by new people and new money. The reincarnated Fiction House favored sparsely dressed girls for its covers and false-sounding names for its authors. Each issue of the new *Jungle Stories* featured a short novel signed John Peter Drummond and introduced by some of the finest blurbs ever concocted:

> It was war to the death! The half-wild white son of Africa against a ruthless, self-made jungle Emperor—with that lost, pampered darling of Civilization as the prize.

> When assagais-wise Masai warriors quailed before the twin-fanged beasts of the Black Vengeance Monster, Ki-Gor knew that the captive Helene was doomed to die ... unless his lion-thewed strength could crush those snarling devil-dogs!

> The leopard-guarded stronghold of M'Mubi-M'ni shook with the muffled drums of death. No man could battle the

Evil-Too-Awful-To-Name and live. But like a berserk jungle killer Ki-Gor stormed forward.

Like Tarzan, Ki-Gor had an upper-class mate and the
added advantage of being able to work witch doctor
magic. Ki-Gor was usually called the Great White Lord
and the attitude toward black men in his adventures and
almost all the jungle pulp stories is at best patronizing.

Besides jungle men, lion men, cave men, dawn men and
similar naked heroes, the pulp magazines also did a brisk
trade in barbarians. Broad-shouldered battle-happy no-
ble savages frequently stalked the pages of magazines
like *Adventure, Argosy, Blue Book* and *Top-Notch,* wield-
ing axes, clubs and swords. The best remembered of the
pulpwood barbarians, and the character who is today still
giving Tarzan competition, is Robert E. Howard's Conan.
Conan first appeared in the December 1932 issue of *Weird
Tales,* a pulp to be covered in more detail further on. L.
Sprague de Camp, who has revived and refurbished
much of the Conan pulp material for paperback publication, describes Howard's barbarian series this way: "As
nearly as such things can be calculated, Conan flourished
about twelve thousand years ago. In this time (according
to Howard) the Western parts of the main continent were
occupied by the Hyborian kingdoms. . . . Conan, a gigantic
adventurer from Commeria, arrived as a youth in the
kingdom of Zamora. For two or three years he made his
living as a thief in Zamora, Corinthia and Nemedia.
Growing tired of this starveling existence, he enlisted as
a mercenary in the armies of Turan. For the next two
years he traveled widely and refined his knowledge of
archery and horsemanship." Conan had several more odd
jobs after that.

Robert E. Howard, a Texan, began turning out large
quantities of pulp stories while still in his teens. Besides
the weird and fantasy markets, he hit many of the action

and adventure magazines. When he wasn't writing for
the pulps he was reading them. The swords and sorcery
facet of his work was much influenced by such writers as
Talbot Munday and Harold Lamb. He borrowed what he
could from both, though he was never able to imitate
their restraint.

Before concocting his super barbarian, Howard had
written of several other blood-thirsty heroes for *Weird
Tales.* In 1928 he introduced Solomon Kane, a 16th Century Puritan adventurer. Kane roamed the world encoun-
tering and overcoming magic and evil. His favorite
stamping ground was Africa where he fought, like many
later Howard protagonists, against sorcery and ferocious
black men. Solomon Kane's conflicts were usually bloody
and hyperthymic.

> He cut her bonds and lifted her tenderly—only to drop her
> again and whirl as a hideous, blood-stained figure of in-
> sanity came leaping and gibbering up the steps. Full upon
> Kane's blade the creature ran, and toppled back into the
> red swirl below, clawing beast-like at its mortal wound.
>
> Then beneath Kane's feet the altar rocked; a sudden
> tremor hurled him to his knees and his horrified eyes be-
> held the Tower of Death sway to and fro. . . . The rest was
> a red nightmare in which Kane's dazed brain refused to
> record all its horrors. It seemed that for screaming crim-
> son centuries he reeled through the narrow winding
> streets where bellowing, screeching demons battled and
> died.

Howard wrote a dozen stories about Kane, alternating
them with tales of heroes more remote in time and more
barbaric in attitude. One such was King Kull, featured in
Weird Tales in the late '20's. These adventures took place,
according to Donald A. Wollheim, "Before Egypt . . . [in]
the darkness of unrecorded time and the ruins of myriad

buried cities and shattered kingdoms, heaped amid the ashes of a thousand lost causes." In addition to Kull there were Bran Mak Morn and Turlogh O'Brien, both Celtic barbarians. O'Brien appears in a story entitled *The Blonde Goddess of Bal-Sagoth* and in this one Howard gets to the grue right in the first paragraph.

Lightning dazzled the eyes of Turlogh O'Brien and his foot slipped in a smear of blood as he staggered on the reeling deck. The clashing of steel rivaled the bellowing of the thunder, and screams of death cut through the roar of waves and wind. The incessant lightning flicker gleamed on the corpses sprawling redly . . .

The parade of skull-splitting barbarians was finally joined by Conan in 1932. He became the most popular character *Weird Tales* ever got hold of. The enormously muscled Conan spent most of his days alternately dallying with lovely princesses and slave girls—

It was a woman who stood staring at them in wonder. She was tall, lithe, shaped like a goddess; clad in a narrow girdle crusted with jewels. A burnished mass of night-black hair set off the whiteness of her ivory body. Her dark eyes, shaded by long dusky lashes, were deep with sensuous mystery. Conan caught his breath at her beauty.

—and struggling against malignant magic and sorcery. The rest of the time he got into fights.

A score of figures faced him, yellow men in purple tunics, with short swords in their hands. As he turned, they surged in on him with hostile cries. He made no attempt to conciliate them. Maddened at the disappearance of his sweetheart, the barbarian reverted to type.
   A snarl of bloodthirsty gratification hummed in his bull-throat as he leaped, and the first attacker, his short sword

overreached by the whistling saber, went down with his brains gushing from his split skull. Wheeling like a cat, Conan caught a descending wrist on his edge, and the hand gripping the short sword flew into the air, scattering a shower of red drops. But Conan had not paused or hesitated. A pantherish twist and shift of his body avoided the blundering rush of two yellow swordsmen, and the blade of one, missing its objective, was sheathed in the breast of the other.

In 1936, Howard, just thirty, killed himself. His stories of Conan, epics of adolescent fantasies and fears, were forgotten for nearly two decades. Then they gradually began coming back into print. In the 1970's the Conan character is more popular than he ever was in his pulp years.

CHAPTER ELEVEN

SUPER SCIENCE

"Matt!" he yelled. "They've got Dottie, in a ship made from our plans. Let's go!"

"Slow down—don't go off half-cocked. What do you plan?"

"Plan! Just chase 'em and kill 'em!"

"Which way did they go?"

"Straight up."

—E.E. Smith,
The Skylark of Space

THE pulp magazines were selling science fiction years before they knew what to call it. Back in the first decades of the century, the Munsey pulpwood magazines were printing stories like "Under the Moons of Mars" and "Beyond The Great Oblivion" and labeling them "different stories." In fact, even after there was a whole magazine offering this kind of different, pseudo-scientific material there was still no agreed-on term. Editor and publisher Hugo Gernsback is credited with first calling science fiction science fiction. This was in 1929, some three years after he'd launched *Amazing Stories*.

The term science fiction came to serve as an umbrella, under which were gathered the many types of imaginative and speculative stories that had been appearing in the general adventure pulps, both scientific romance and scientific speculation. Science fiction could accommodate planet-hopping adventure, satiric thoughts about the future, trips through time to the past. Spacemen and monstrous aliens, fragile princesses, mad scientists, absent-minded professors and dedicated researchers. Hymns in praise of technology and dire warnings about the perils of the machine. Utopia and anti-Utopia. Hard science, pseudo science and crackpot science. All in all, the science fiction pulp was potentially more catholic in scope than most other genre pulps. In the first decade or so of science fiction magazines this wide potential was overlooked more often than it was taken advantage of. The emphasis tended to be, particularly in the 1930's, on action and heroes.

Before there were science fiction pulps, the Munsey magazines—*Argosy, All-Story* and *Cavalier*—ran a sizeable amount of science fiction material, due in good part to the editorial philosophy of senior editor Robert H. Davis. The favored type came to be the scientific romance, the story mixing action with a little technology and a little love interest. The star performer here, from 1912 onward, was Edgar Rice Burroughs. After "Under the Moons of Mars," Burroughs turned out several more John Carter of Mars adventures, and in 1914 branched with "At the Earth's Core," which took its hero to Pellucidar. Finally, in 1931, Burroughs got around to another planet and did "Pirates of Venus" for *Argosy*.

During the ascendency of Burroughs, several other authors mined similar ground for Munsey. George Allan

England, Charles B. Stilson, J.U. Giesy, A. Merritt and Otis Adelbert Kline all wrote scientific romances, using remote places and planets and a smattering of science. Kline, who made a career of following in Burroughs' footsteps, had his own Mars and Venus series running. Eventually the solar system would be used up and the galactic space opera would supersede the scientific romance. But first there had to be Hugo Gernsback.

Hugo Gernsback was much too eclectic in mind to stick to any limiting definition of what a science fiction pulp had to be. A man who would write science fiction serials for a radio repair magazine obviously cared little for categories or for a narrow view of what was appropriate. And so *Amazing Stories,* the pioneer SF magazine he started in 1926, was somewhat wider-ranging than many of its immediate imitators. Gernsback was in his forties when he became the father of the science fiction magazine. A native of Luxembourg, Gernsback had come to the United States in 1904. He was an electrical engineer by trade and hoped to find in America a market for some of the things he'd invented—or was thinking about inventing. Gernsback had little luck finding a buyer for his version of the dry cell battery. His attempts to market batteries on his own failed, too, and he next formed an electrical equipment company. "For this venture," Gernsback's frequent biographer Sam Moskowitz tells us, "which was to become the first mail-order radio house in the world, Gernsback designed the first home radio set in history. . . . This amateur unit contained a transmitter as well as a receiver, since no commercial radio stations existed at the time."

In 1908, Gernsback, drawing on the experience he'd gained putting out catalogues for his various unsuccessful businesses, went into magazine publishing and issued *Modern Electrics*, the first magazine devoted to radio. Gernsback had had an interest in speculative writing

since a book on the possibility of life on Mars had excited
him into a fever at the age of nine. So in 1911 when he
found himself with some pages to fill in *Modern Electrics*
he began a science fiction novel. The story had the catchy
title "Ralph 124C41+." "It was negligible as a piece of
fiction," observes Isaac Asimov, "but its plot provided the
frame on which to hang Gernsback's own vision of the
future. He foresaw countless innovations of the decades
to follow with amazing accuracy: night baseball, vending
machines, metal foil, radar and television, among others.
He was, in fact, the first writer to use the word 'television.' " While this romance of the year 2660 didn't cause
a big jump in the circulation of the radio magazine, it
didn't scare off any readers. And Gernsback began to use
more fiction, all of it scientific or futuristic. Finally, in
1928, he was ready to try a whole magazine of what he
was at that point calling "scientifiction" and *Amazing
Stories* resulted. The first issue reached the stands, un-
heralded and unadvertised, graced with a bright yellow
cover by Frank R. Paul. Paul, a former New Jersey newspaper cartoonist, went on producing his intricate and
primitive paintings (looking like what might result if you
programmed a computer to be Grandma Moses) for
Amazing for the next twenty years. The contributors to
that first issue included H. G. Wells, Jules Verne and Edgar Allan Poe. Gradually Gernsback made enough money
to allow him to use fewer reprints and more living authors. He attracted a varied group of new writers:
Fletcher Pratt, John W. Campbell, Stanton Coblentz, Jack
Williamson and E.E. Smith.

Edward E. Smith was one of the major engineers of the
space opera. Smith was born in 1890 and grew up in the
Northwest. He majored in chemical engineering and in
1919, with the help of money from relatives and spare
time jobs, he got his Ph.D. This hard-earned degree im-
pressed him and when he began appearing in the pulp

magazines he used it the way *Adventure* contributors used their military rank, always signing himself, Edward E. Smith, Ph.D. His first novel was nearly as long in coming as his degree. Before the first World War, when Smith was living in Michigan and working as a cereal chemist for a donut concern, he'd started collaborating on a scientific adventure novel with the wife of an old school friend named Garby. It took the two of them two years to get a third of the book finished. After that Smith wrote on alone, finally finishing the novel around 1920. The next seven years he spent trying to sell "The Skylark of Space."

At last, in 1928, *Amazing Stories* bought Smith's novel, paying him $125. He split the money with Mrs. Garby. The Skylark was an enormous space ship, built to cruise the galaxy. "This novel was the first to deal to any extent with the incredible power to be had from the release of intra-atomic energy and its application to space travel," reports science fiction historian Alva Rogers. "The Skylark and its passengers tour the universe, encountering all sorts of wild and wonderful adventures, strange beings, and creatures, and marvels beyond compare. . . . To the fan of an earlier generation, a novel by E.E. Smith, Ph.D. was an adventure in reading scarcely to be equaled. The sweep of a Smith novel that used the entire galaxy (and then some) as a stage, the slashing space battles so well described, the super-human qualities of Richard Seaton and Martin Crane who (with a little help here and there from friendly alien races) overcome the most inconceivable obstacles, and that wicked but delightfully wonderful villain, Dr. Marc 'Blackie' DuQuesne, all combined to enthrall the reader."

"The Skylark of Space" is basically a chase novel, with inventor Seaton hunting down Blackie DuQuesne, a fellow scientist who's gone bad and stolen not only

Seaton's ideas but his sweetheart. Instead of the horses or
automobiles or speedboats of silent movie serials, Smith's
characters use giant spacecraft. The style of writing, possibly due to the influence of Mrs. Garby, mixes scientific
jargon with 1915 collegiate slang, producing such passages as :

> Seaton and Crane drove the Skylark at high acceleration
> in the direction indicated by the unwavering compass,
> each man taking a twelve-hour trick at the board.
>
> The Skylark justified the faith of her builders, and the
> two inventors, with an exultant certainty of success, flew
> out beyond man's wildest imaginings. Had it not been for
> the haunting fear for Dorothy's safety, the journey would
> have been one of pure triumph, and even that anxiety did
> not preclude a profound joy in the enterprise.
>
> "If that misguided ape thinks he can pull a stunt like
> that and get away with it he's got another think coming,"
> Seaton declared, after making a reading on the other ship
> after a few days of flight. "He went off half-cocked for sure
> this time, and we've got him where the hair is short. Only
> about a hundred light-years now."

Pulp readers of the late 1920's fell under the spell of
Smith and admired his ability to write of action "on a
cosmic scale." Smith, who kept working full time in the
donut business, wrote sequels in his off hours. "Skylark
Three" came in 1930 and "Skylark of Valeron" in 1934. By
then he was also selling, at slightly better word rates, to
Astounding. For this last pulp he conceived a new series.
This, dealing with Kimball Kinnison, the Grey Lensman,
began in 1937. Kinnison belongs to the Galactic Patrol,
having graduated first in his class from Patrol Academy,
and works as an interstellar policeman. The Lensman
novels are chases, too, with Kinnison hurtling through
the galaxy on the trail of a vast conspiracy known only as
Boskone.

The kind of novel that Smith introduced in *Amazing* in 1928 helped set a pattern that would persist until the '40's, as did the 1928 *Amazing* novel by Philip Francis Nowlan which introduced the character Buck Rogers. 1928 was a good year for Hugo Gernsback. But in 1929 he had to declare bankruptcy and sell his magazine.

That same year, *Astounding* came along. A publication of the Clayton Company, its original and complete name was *Astounding Stories Of Super-Science*. This new science fiction pulp was "unabashedly an action adventure magazine." Its publication came about, as its first editor Harry Bates remembers it, this way: "At the time there were, I think, thirteen Clayton magazines. . . . Routinely each month, the editors of these and the other magazines bought eye-catching pictures for the covers of their next issues, the engravers made plates from them, and the printer furnished final proofs of them, all thirteen assembled rectangularly on a single large sheet of paper. . . . Now, there were blank places on this sheet. The proofs occupied places arranged in four rows of four columns each, only thirteen of the sixteen places being filled. This meant that month after month three of the sixteen places would stare empty at Clayton, in effect reproving him for not having three *more* magazines so that they need *not* be empty. I venture upon certainty when I say that Clayton on looking at this sheet would often have these particular money-lustful thoughts: 'If I had sixteen magazines I'd get the three additional covers cheap . . . the paper for the covers, now being wasted, would be free.' " Armed with his extrasensory hunches about what Clayton was thinking, and the armful of back issues of *Amazing* he'd been studying, Bates approached the publisher. "I pumped myself full of combativeness and charged into Clayton's office. It was as easy as pie! There'd be an action-adventure *Astounding Stories of Super-Science*! I was to get right to work on it."

Besides making up the new magazine for Clayton, Bates also created one of *Astounding*'s early popular heroes; the space opera star, Hawk Carse. In his history of the magazine Alva Rogers describes this series as epitomizing "the Clayton Astounding type of science fiction more nearly than any other stories . . . With steel nerves, raw courage, and flashing rayguns, the Hawk and his faithful companion, the giant Negro Friday, ranged the Solar system in deadly pursuit of their great enemy, the evil space pirate Dr. Ku Sui, whose one aim was to dominate the Solar system . . . The stories contained just about every cliche and stereotyped character to be found in what later came to be known as 'space opera.' " The Space Hawk adventures were signed Anthony Gilmore and their prose, turned out by Bates in collaboration with a man named D.W. Hall, helped inspire a decade of space adventures:

> Hawk Carse's icy poise in times of emotional stress never failed to amaze friends and enemies alike. Most of them said he had no nerves, and therefore was not human. This estimate, of course, was foolish: Carse was human, perhaps too human, as was amply indicated by the several objects of his life. It was probably an inward vanity that made him stand composed in the face of probable death; vanity and the example of leadership that once, for instance, led him to actually file his fingernails when trapped and hotly besieged, with the hiss of ray-guns in the hands of fighting men all around.
>
> And so he stood now within his spacesuit—cool, his face graven, while the yellow tendrils carpeted the entire cabin, penetrated the twin banks of instruments on each side and clouded the bow windows and miniscreen until outside vision was completely cut off. . . .

Even with the help of the Space Hawk and others like him, William Clayton couldn't escape the financial collapse brought about by the Depression and some complex internal office problems. He went under, selling off what magazine titles he could. Street & Smith bought some of them, *Astounding* included.

Hugo Gernsback was at it again. But, like many other inventors, he never had much luck with his own inventions. The '30's were filled with the sound of one Gernsback science fiction magazine after another falling over. *Science Wonder Stories* thrived for only a dozen issues, from the spring of 1929 to the spring of 1930. *Air Wonder Stories*, which was devoted to the future of air and space travel, expired at the same time after an even shorter career. The warm months of 1930 also saw the end of *Scientific Detective Monthly*. This specialized magazine was supposed to be devoted to detective stories with a science fiction element. Actually it was another Gernsback grabbag, which reprinted old adventures of the 1910 scientific sleuth Craig Kennedy and even serialized a Philo Vance novel. There were, though, a few authentic SF touches. Sam Moskowitz tells us, "a new scientific detective, *The Electrical Man* , Miller Rand, was created for the May, 1930 issue by Neil R. Jones . . . The electrical man wears all bulletproof clothes including his mask, gloves and socks. His clothes are electrified, stunning any man who touches him, and he gets his power transmitted to him by radio."

Gernsback next merged most of his fallen titles into one magazine and named that *Wonder Stories*. The first few issues were thin and on a better quality paper. The magazine then reverted to pulpwood stock and lasted for nearly six years. By 1936, with only a few thousand readers still faithful, Gernsback gave up *Wonder Stories*. Ned Pines' Standard Company bought it and Leo Margulies became the magazine's new editorial director. If you've been reading this book

straight through, you can guess what Margulies did next.
He changed the name to *Thrilling Wonder Stories.*

The magazine now became even more aggressively
juvenile than it had been under Gernsback. Monsters
tripped over exclamation points on the covers and in the
illustrations. In the stories spacemen saved the world, if
not indeed the whole universe, several times a month.
There was more emphasis on series characters, heroes
who could be followed, and collected, from issue to issue.
There were immortal men, galactic big game hunters
and an assortment of space mercenaries and patrolmen.
While this breathless heroic approach worked well in the
pulps, it proved to work even better in the emerging
comic books. In 1938, Major Malcolm Wheeler-Nicholson's fumbling comic book imitations of the pulps had
become million-circulation properties. The dapper major
had gone broke by this time, but the people who took over
his company were growing rich and they owned Superman. When the rising Superman-DC company decided to
expand they hired, significantly, a good part of Margulies'
staff away from him. Editorial personnel like Mort Weis-
inger and Jack Schiff and staff writers like Alfred Bester
and H.L. Gold.

As the 1930's ended, a rash of new science fiction pulps
broke out on the newsstands. Leo Margulies added *Startling Stories* late in 1938. This was initially edited by Weis-
inger, who also had a hand in the new *Captain Future*
magazine, which appeared two years later. SF historian
Sam Moskowitz, who has written more about science
fiction than Prescott wrote about Mexico, says, "It came
about this way. While attending the First World Science
Fiction Convention in New York City, July 2, 1939, Leo
Margulies . . . after listening to the proceedings for a few
hours, emitted his now famous line: 'I didn't think you
fans could be so damn sincere.' He followed it with action,
plotting on the spot a new science-fiction magazine. It

was to be called *Captain Future* . . . There must be a superscientist hero. There must also be aides: a robot and an android and, of course, a beautiful female assistant. Each story must be a crusade to bring to justice an arch villain; and, in each novel, the hero must be captured and escape three times."

The *Captain Future* pulp hit the stands early in 1940 and appeared every three months thereafter, offering such adventures as "Calling Captain Future," "Captain Future's Challenge" and "The Triumph of Captain Future." All but three of the nearly two dozen Captain Future novels were written by Edmond Hamilton. Hamilton had been writing cosmic adventures and space operas for the science fiction pulps since 1926, the first year there were science fiction pulps. His hero, Curt Newton, better known as Captain Future, survived in the pulp quarterly for a little over four years and after that made two comebacks in *Startling Stories*. He expired for good in 1951.

Another emerging pulp in the early '40's was Fiction House's *Planet Stories*, combining the spirit of Space Hawk with the decorations of *Spicy Detective*. This caught an audience a bit further along in adolescence. In the 1940's the *Thrilling-Startling* twins joined *Planet* in sporting covers that combined interplanetery action with dishevelled girls. A new species of menace developed on the bright covers of the lesser SF pulps—a googly-eyed alien who was both inhospitable and horny. The bug-eyed monster, or BEM, was so visible twenty-five to thirty years ago that most middle-aged people in the United States still automatically think of a BEM at the mention of science fiction. Other pulps that followed briefly in the early years of World War II were *Comet Stories, Cosmic Stories, Astonishing Stories, Future Science Fiction* and *Super Science*. The Munsey Company, reduced by financial necessity to living more and more in the past with reprints, introduced *Famous Fantastic Mysteries* and *Fantastic Novels* to draw on the backlog. The Munsey Company was gone by the end of 1942 and Popular Publications took over the two magazines and the backlog of old scientific romances.

Meanwhile *Amazing Stories* had moved to Chicago and grown fat. The Ziff-Davis company bought the title in 1938 and, for lack of anything better to do, gave the editorship to Raymond A. Palmer, age 28. Palmer had been a fan of the magazine, and of all science fiction, since his boyhood days in Milwaukee. In 1930 he'd sold his first SF story and in 1933 he organized something called the Jules Verne Prize Club with the intended purpose of giving loving cups to the science fiction authors voted best by the club. Besides his fan and writer components, Palmer had a good percentage of P.T. Barnum in him. This was a combination of qualities well suited to help the slowly sinking *Amazing.* Palmer, in typical Palmer style, has said of his taking over as editor, "Here at last I had it in my power to do to my old hobby what I had always had the driving desire to do to it. I had in my hands the power to change, to destroy, to create, to remake, at my own discretion." What Palmer brought forth was a thick flamboyant pulp (it eventually swelled to over 250 pages), aimed at adolescent boys and, possibly, superstitious old ladies. The circulation is said to have quickly risen from about 25,000 to nearly 200,000 under Palmer.

Relying on old time professionals and young fans for contributions, Palmer also searched Chicago for new writers he could use. When all else failed, he wrote chunks of *Amazing* himself. A typical issue would contain stories by Edgar Rice Burroughs, Festus Pragnell, John York Cabot, P.F. Costello and Thornton Ayre. Half of them were actually Palmer and his cohorts in disguise. The Palmer art department was a fairly disparate operation. It included the venerable Burroughs illustrator, J.

Allen St. John, a painter of Catholic calendars, Robert Gibson Jones, and a cartoonist who drew a strip called *The Toodles Family*, Rod Ruth. In 1939 Ziff-Davis added *Fantastic Adventures* to its line. Originally a tall thin magazine, *Fantastic* was also Palmer's and featured a B-movie mixture of SF and fantasy. Here Palmer gave his readers such characters as the Golden Amazon, "an amazing girl with the strength of ten," Lancelot Biggs the space navigator and the Whispering Gorilla—"because he knew too much, Steven Carpenter was exiled to Africa. Then he was murdered. But he came back, determined to exact vengeance, as a gorilla!"

Raymond A. Palmer's most memorable contribution to the field of pulp science fiction was the Shaver Mystery. Richard S. Shaver lived in a small town in Pennsylvania and believed in Lemurians. Commencing with "I Remember Lemuria" in the March, 1945 issue of *Amazing*, Shaver's accounts of his experiences with and theories about the refugees of the Atlantis-like Lemuria became a regular series. "The tales were Palmer's expansions of briefer drafts by a Pennsylvania welder," explains Martin Gardner in his history of quackery, *In The Name Of Science*. "Drawing on his 'racial memories' Shaver described in great detail the activities of a midget race of degenerates called 'Deros' who live in huge caverns beneath the surface of the earth. By means of telepathy and secret rays the Deros are responsible for most of earth's catastrophes—wars, fires, airplane crashes, ship wrecks, and nervous breakdowns." Television writer Howard Browne was an associate editor at *Amazing* then and this is his account of how the Shaver Mystery got started: "Early in the '40's, a letter came to us from Dick Shaver purporting to reveal the 'truth' about a race of freaks, called 'Deros', living under the surface of the earth. Ray Palmer read it, handed it to me for comment. I read a third of it, tossed it in the waste basket. Ray, who loved to show his editors a trick or two about the business, fished it out of the basket, ran it in *Amazing*—and a flood of mail poured in from readers who insisted every word of it was true because *they'd* been plagued by Deros for years. Palmer traveled to Pennsylvania (if I remember right) to talk to Shaver, found him sitting on reams of stuff he'd written about the Deros, bought every bit of it and contracted for more. I thought it was about the sickest crap I'd run into. Palmer ran it and doubled the circulation of *Amazing* within four months. When I took over from Palmer, in 1949, I put an abrupt end to the 'Mystery' —writing off over $7,000 worth of scripts."

Fortunately for science fiction, not all editors courted the lunatic fringe and the youth market. Or at least not the early teen age side of the youth market. After some changes in title, format and editorship, *Astounding* came under the editorial control of John W. Campbell in 1937. Though in later years Campbell was to reveal an almost Palmer-like fascination with quackery (and champion such dubious causes as Dianetics and dowsing), his taste in stories was consistently better than any of his contemporaries in the '30's. He seems to have had, then, a sense of humor as well. Campbell had been writing science fiction himself since his student days at M.I.T. His work had been printed in *Amazing, Wonder Stories* and *Astounding.* These efforts were space operas, filled with super-heroics. In fact, Aarn Munro, the incredible hero of Campbell's 1934 *Astounding* super science epic, "The Mightiest Machine," was so strong and simplistic that Street & Smith tried to turn him into a comic book character a few years later. But there was another side to Campbell, and under the penname Don A. Stuart he wrote quieter, more speculative stories. As he got older the level of the work in *Astounding* seemed to mature along with him. "By 1938, there came a new turning point," says Isaac Asimov, whose own career as a science fiction writer was to begin that year. "Campbell realized that the readership of science fiction had grown older and more sophisticated. He demanded stories from writers who knew something about science and engineering, and of the way in which scientists and engineers thought and worked. Under Campbell's guidance, science fiction entered its 'golden age' of the late 1930's and early 1940's, during which many of the science fiction writers of today got their start—e.g.: Robert A. Heinlein, L. Sprague de Camp, Theodore Sturgeon, Arthur C. Clarke, Poul Anderson, A.E. van Vogt, Lester del Ray, Eric Frank Russell, and Clifford D. Simak."

The new trends in science fiction spread in the 1940's. In 1945 there was Hiroshima, that terrible monument to the best and worst of science. It was difficult for science fiction writers to be satisfied after that with simply making technological predictions that might come true—and impossible to write about galactic heroics with atomic ray guns. Even *Thrilling Wonder Stories* grew up and readers found Ray Bradbury, Philip Jose Farmer, John D. MacDonald and Henry Kuttner, to name a few, thinking about the future of people. Heroes seemed less of a necessity.

CHAPTER TWELVE

ODDS & ENDS

You can sell anything once.

—Old advertising saying

A year or so ago I spent an afternoon interviewing artist Walter Baumhofer in his studio on Long Island. Taking time out from the large sedate 4-H Club calendar illustration he was at work on, Baumhofer talked about the '30's when he'd been painting sixty to seventy pulp covers a year. He'd retained color proofs of a good many of the covers, particularly those he'd done for Harold Hersey. Hersey had been an editor with the Clayton company and had then started his own pulp venture in the late 1920's. Hersey was one of the publishers who felt the public was always ready for a new title or a new kind of pulp magazine. Which is why Baumhofer was able to show me cover proofs from such ephemeral magazines as *Courtroom Stories, Fire Fighters, Western Outlaws, The Danger Trail, Speakeasy Stories, Racketeer Stories, Speed Stories, Headquarters Stories, Dragnet Magazine, Prison Stories, New York Stories* and a considerable number more. The Hersey attitude was common in the heyday of the pulps and it produced some interesting strains.

One of the oddest varieties was the horror magazine. The pioneer here was *Weird Tales*, a perennially tottering Chicago-based pulp. The first issue appeared early in 1923 with a cover illustrating that month's featured story, *Ooze*. A rallying point for every sort of monster, ghost and fiend, *Weird Tales* was edited in the '20's and '30's by Farnsworth Wright. Wright was a tall, bent man, ailing. An ex-reporter with a fondness for reciting dirty limericks, he remained with the magazine until his death in 1940. *Weird Tales* was always in financial trouble and never made anybody, even its publishers, rich. Wright stayed because of affection. "He loved the florid, the exotic, the richly phrased, the high flight of fancy," says an early contributor. "He believed in his magazine." The pulp, in its nearly thirty years, offered readers a smorgasbord of horrors, both traditional and unusual—grinning ghouls, grinning mummies, haunted mansions, midnight visitors, mist monsters, mutations, tomb dwellers, tree men, unicorns, vampires, werewolves, whistling corpses, witch doctors, wolfwomen, yellow dooms, beasts, beetles, germs, giants, golden spiders, graveyard rats and black abbots, black adders, black castles, black druids, black hounds, black kisses, black masses, black sorceries, etc.

There were contributions from a profusion of authors, both living and dead. Early issues contained reprints of Daniel Defoe, Bulwer-Lytton, Conan Doyle and Edgar Allan Poe along with new material by Otis Adelbert Kline, the Burroughs-doppleganger, as well as Austin Hall, E. Hoffman Price, Vincent Starrett, Frank Owen and C.M.

Eddy, Jr. Eddy gained a brief and circumscribed fame in 1924 with a weird tale called "The Loved Dead." The central character practiced necrophilia and shared his experiences with the reader—"One morning Mr. Gresham came much earlier than usual—came to find me stretched out upon a cold slab deep in ghoulish slumber, my arms wrapped around the stark stiff, naked body of a fetid corpse." This story generated denunciations, indignation, suppressions and publicity for *Weird Tales.* You can't build a large circulation solely with necrophilia fans, but the new notoriety of the faltering pulp was sufficient to attract enough new readers to allow it to stay in operation.

Two other significant *Weird Tales* contributors emerged in the middle 1920's, both of them haunted and reclusive men. They were Clark Ashton Smith and H.P. Lovecraft. Smith, who did his hiding in the California woodlands, first appeared with poetry and then, in 1928, began a series of wispy tales he referred to as "stories of exotic beauty, horror, terror, strangeness, irony and satire." Smith set his stories in imaginary lands and mythical kingdoms and was extremely fond of gibberish in his titles: "The Maze of Maal Dweb," "The Weird of Auoosl Wuthoqquan," "The Vaults of Yoh-Vombis," etc. Smith was much admired by the magazine's readers and according to Lin Carter, who edited a recent collection of Smith's work, he was a source of inspiration to A.E. van Vogt, Jack Vance, Fritz Leiber, Ray Bradbury and Theodore Sturgeon.

The Clark Ashton Smith prose is circuitous stuff, straining to be pretty, and his tales abound with passages such as:

Long had the wasting summer pastures its suns, like fiery red stallions, on the dun hills that crouched before the Mykrasian Mountains in wild easternmost Cincor. The

peak-fed torrents were become tenuous threads or far-sun-
dered, fallen pools; the granite boulders were shaled by
the heat; the bare earth was cracked and creviced; and the
low, meager grasses were scared even to the roots.

So it occurred that the boy Xeethra, tending the black
and piebald goats of his uncle Pornos, was obliged to follow his charges farther each day on the combes and hill-
tops, etc.

H.P. Lovecraft, who shut himself up in Rhode Island for
most of his life, also labored over his prose, striving to
sound like a voice out of an earlier and better century. His
first *Weird Tales* story was published in October, 1923,
and most of his best remembered work was done for the
magazine over the next ten years or so. Lovecraft was
preoccupied with death and decay and the other shocks
the flesh is heir to. For him, the family circle was a source
of dreadful fancies, and his stories return again and
again to the horrors of incest and inbreeding, of heredi-
tary taints and family dooms, of fantastic misalliances
and grotesque matings. Lovecraft took to monumental
extremes the child's notion that the bogey man will get
you if you don't watch out, fashioning a mythology about
ancient gods and babbling aliens.

Though much of Lovecraft's work is spoiled now by an
unwitting silliness, some few of his stories—"Cool Air,"
"The Rats in the Walls"—still have the effect intended.
Some effort has been made in recent writings about Lovecraft to demonstrate that he was actually a detached and
cool professional who wrote weird tales for a living. But
it is evident in his better stories that he himself was really
frightened by what he was writing about, and by what he
could never quite bring himself to write about.

In its three decades *Weird Tales* also gave room to such
writers as Seabury Quinn, C.L. Moore, Henry Kutter, Robert Bloch, August Derleth, Fritz Leiber and Ray Brad-

bury, who, like Lovecraft, used the horror story to exorcise his childhood traumas. There were also early contributions from Marc Schorer, Tennessee Williams and Val Lewton. Later, in the 1940's, Lewton produced a string of "B" horror films for RKO—*The Cat People, Isle Of The Dead, I Walked With A Zombie*—that are still well thought of and frequently shown.

It was a series of movies of the '30's that helped inspire the magazines that finally came along to join *Weird Tales* in the horror category. Popular Publications' *Horror, Terror* and *Dime Mystery*, fifteen cents each, hit the stands about the same time the new wave of horror talkies—*Dracula, The Invisible Man, The Mummy, Frankenstein*—were pulling customers into motion picture houses. This trio of pulps was under the supervision of Rogers Terrill, who had been an editor with Fiction House before joining Popular. Terrill, who also masterminded the calamities that befell Operator 5 and the Spider, apparently had little affection for the horror story and no high opinion of the kind of readers he was out to attract. When asking Frederick Davis about his work for these magazines, I referred to them as bizarre, and he replied, "Strangely enough Rog used exactly this word when telling us what he wanted for them. I once asked him to give me his definition of the difference between horror and terror . . . He said that horror is the emotion you feel when you see something awful happening to someone else; terror is what you feel when the something is about to happen to you." In *Dime Mystery, Terror* and *Horror*, both what happened to somebody else and what happened to you could be counted on to be perverse. Bruno Fischer, who, under the penname Russell Gray, was the star contributor to the Terrill trinity, says of the magazines: "They were of course lurid magazines—sex, sadism, horror, terror, mood."

The opposition soon followed Popular and for a time in

the '30's there was a short row of bizarre pulps on the stands. A.A. Wyn gave it a brief try with *Ace Mystery*. Martin Goodman, later to bring forth the Marvel comics line, also entered the field with *Uncanny Tales* and *Mystery Tales*. And Leo Margulies, whose devotion to the word thrilling never diminished, produced *Thrilling Mystery*. Popular fought back by adding, in 1937, *Strange Detective Mysteries*. As the 1930's progressed, these pulps moved increasingly away from the old dark house and increasingly closer to the old dark perversions. "Popular continued to feature the weird menace story, at the same time modifying it," writes Bob Jones in a study of the horror and terror pulps. "The covers provide a visual record of the newly emerging theme. Early issues had the heroine pursued down dark corridors, or hiding in dank dungeons . . . There was little eroticism in these scenes. As the 1938 period approached, a sex-sadistic sophistication crept in. More and more nudes appeared. Now the girls were being tortured by such contrivances as buzz saws, boiling and freezing water, electric drills . . . The wild staring look in the fiends' eyes was seemingly replaced by one of lust."

Stories and novelets now terrified readers with such titles as "The Goddess Of Crawling Horrors," "The Beast Wants Me," "Venus-Slave Of Horror," and "The Thing That Darkness Spawned." And some very odd things happened to the people in the stories. For instance, June Daly is almost torn to bits by the Thin Men of Id and is only saved in the nick of time by a midget private detective. In "Red Hand Of Kali", hero Moriarity O'Moore expects to find a slip of a girl in a darkened bedroom and instead finds himself in bed with the dread tic polonga snake. Or take Landa Maine, whose heredity problem was explained in the story title "I Am The Tiger Girl." Then there were helpless maidens assaulted by lascivious goatmen, small town girls attacked by voodoo snake men, dancing girls hypnotized by lustful Chinese illusionists. Young couples had their honeymoons blighted by putty-skinned cavemen or by inquisitorial octogenarians. There is considerable torture carried on in the latter day horror pulps and a great deal of fascination with pain. Deformities, maimings, disembowelings are all presented in explicit, often loving detail. You'll have to take my word for this, since this is one genre I am refraining from quoting. Various civic pressures, and the real horrors of the new World War put an end to most of the horror pulps by the early '40's. Fortunately, unlike what has happened in the case of the relatively literate *Weird Tales*, none of the material from any of the weird menace pulps has been preserved in books or elsewhere, and the gruesome stuff is now as defunct as a mad doctor at the end of a *Dime Mystery* novelet.

The fictional sports hero was never as popular in the pulps as he had been in the more innocent years of Frank Merriwell and the *Tip Top Weekly*. Street & Smith launched their *Sport Story* magazine in 1923, and it attained a healthy, though not outstanding, circulation of 150,000 a month. In 1928, Bill Kofoed talked Fiction House into letting him edit a magazine devoted to boxing fiction, *Fight Stories*. This magazine, like many of the jock pulps, mixed fiction and articles. Novelets and short stories were blended with articles on "How To Develop A Knockout Punch," and sports commentary by columnists like Hype Igoe and Jack Kofoed. Popular Publications came up with a ten cent product in the early '30's and called it *Dime Sports*. A typical 1935 issue featured a baseball novelet, a crew story, a tennis story, a boxing story and a hockey story. Margulies and Pines offered an economical line of sports pulps, too, one of which was, of course, called *Thrilling Sports*. From the '20's to the '40's, sports fans could also find what they were looking for in *Baseball Stories, Exciting Football, Popular Sports* and *Super Sports*.

Love pulps sold handsomely, but produced no heroes or series characters. Street & Smith invented the modern love story magazine, after several years of trying to think up a magazine version of their romantic dime novels. They had, says Quentin Reynolds in his company history, "tried it once in 1913, but the ineptly named *Women's Stories* failed to catch on." Finally in 1920 they hired Amita Fairgrieve, "a woman of charm and editorial acumen," and she gave them *Love Story*. The first issue came out in 1921 and included a novelet, "A Fatal Temptation," credited to Bertha M. Clay. The original bearer of that penname, an English lady named Mrs. Brame, was long since dead and gone, but Bertha M. Clay love novels had been so successful, Street & Smith refused to let her die. It says something for the lady readers of those early post-war years that the name Bertha M. Clay could suggest romance to them. In 1929, an ex-dress model named Daisy Bacon took over as editor of *Love Story*. The circulation now climbed from 100,000 to over half a million. Because, Quentin Reynolds tells us, "Daisy Bacon, with the zeal of a crusader, undertook to defy the customs of the whirlwind '20's. . . . She believed, contrary to the opinion of the critics, that there was still a huge audience which wanted straight old fashioned romance. She felt that sentiment and femininity were due for a revival." Daisy Bacon revived sentiment just as Wall Street fell apart. More sentimental entertainment did come back into fashion and *Love Story* benefited.

Love Story became the most valuable magazine property Street & Smith had in the '30's. They also, with Daisy Bacon in charge, gave the sentimental public *Real Love, Romantic Range* and *Pocket Love*. "The appeal of the love pulps was not illicit sex," as one historian puts it. "Their heroines assiduously defended their virginity even though they drank and sometimes spent the night in a bachelor's apartment." The love pulps were portable soap operas and most publishers added them to their lists as items guaranteed to sell. There were love magazines called *All Story Love, Exciting Love, Gay Love, Ideal Love, New Love* and *Thrilling Love*. This last was an idea of Leo Margulies.

Before the pulp magazines declined and fell, some editor or publisher had put forth a title devoted to almost anything you can think of. There were *Oriental Stories, Dr. Death, Railroad Magazine,* a pulp called *The Wizard* that starred a financial manipulator, *Foreign Legion Adventures*, a pulp called *Big Chief Western* with nothing but Indian stories, *Fifth Column Stories* and even *Zeppelin Stories*. Then, abruptly, there weren't any pulps at all.

CHAPTER THIRTEEN

PENNY A WORD

NOBODY noticed it at the time, but the pulp magazine was one of the casualties of the second World War. The mystery men chuckling in their capes and the bronze geniuses leaping out of penthouses didn't fit very well in the world as it was after Hitler and Hiroshima. By 1946, though there was still a large public for cheap thrills, they were beginning to want them in new shapes and new formats. "The paper back book had offered itself as an alternative," explains a history of popular magazines. "The comic book, and later television, provided the same sort of romantic and adventurous escape . . . Then, too, during and immediately after World War II, publishers of pulps were hit especially hard by swiftly rising production costs, which increased 72 percent between the end of 1944 and mid-1947. Their revenue was no longer enough to support them." So a combination of economic factors, a restless and, to some extent, more sophisticated public and new competition combined to do in the pulps. Some of the publishers folded up completely, others switched to slick paper magazines. A few found out how, as Kellogg's has always been able to do, to package corn in new ways. By the early 1950's, as the Eisenhower years dawned, the pulps were gone.

In the course of doing this book I accumulated a great many firsthand reminiscences from writers, editors and artists who worked in the pulp field in the days when the magazines flourished. This final chapter is made up of these remembrances and is meant to serve as a sort of oral, though typographical, history of what it was like then.

NORMAN DANIELS: *I know what you're after, but there just isn't anything glamorous about writing in any medium. I went to Columbia and Northwestern, did a year of medical school, went broke and got a job as an insurance investigator. Dorothy Daniels, my wife, decided to try writing and I tried my hand at short story writing for the pulps. This was in the mid 1930's. I sold the first story I ever wrote, sold the second and decided this was for me. I didn't sell any more for a year. Then I began to creep slowly into the business. Before long, I was doing a number of contract novels, the 45,000 features used in the pulps in those days. I wrote G-Men, The Phantom Detective, The Candid Camera Kid, The Black Bat, Nick Carter, Doc Savage . . . I've forgotten how many and their titles. I wrote under so many names, I had to keep a file so I'd know who was who when I wrote the by-line.*

FREDERICK NEBEL: *The only* Black Mask *writers I knew well at the time were Hammett and Whitfield: we* *spent a lot of time together socially and I don't recall that we ever talked about Joseph Shaw's influence as an editor. We were too busy clowning around in bars to talk shop. Besides, we never read one another's published work. I did read* The Maltese Falcon, *but that was about a year after it appeared in book form. Hammett and I got stoned one night and I woke up the next morning with an autographed copy. The inscription reads: "To Fred Nebel, in memory of the night of the cloud-burst when we were companions under the umbrella." This referred to a cloudless, starlit night when we strode up Lexington from 37th Street to Grand Central Terminal under an open umbrella, checked the umbrella (insisting that it remain open) and went into the Oyster Bar for some kind of shell food. We returned to the apartment in 37th with the umbrella still open. The idea seemed to be (there was a small bet) that no one would pay any attention to us. No one did.*

RICHARD WORMSER: *With great acumen, I started my own financial news bureau in June of 1929. By 1932, I had had to add commercial and industrial news to my line, there being virtually no finance, and was, in fact New York correspondent for sixteen trade papers.... One by one they went out of business, couldn't pay me, or slowly decreased their size until a monthly check would be in pennies, since I was paid by the line. Early in 1932, Street & Smith decided to get out a low-grade news magazine, inspired by the financial success of* Time. *They turned the editing over to Lon Murray ... He didn't have an ex-newsman on his staff. In fact, no one at S&S had ever handled news. Frank Cockrell, who had been selling Lon a good many sports and college stories, took me down there and I was put on as rewrite man and assistant editor. The news magazine, called* Headlines, *failed almost at once. After almost eighty years, the S&S personnel were not mentally geared to get news out before it* *staled. We would print our theory of a crime, and the police would have it solved and the criminal convicted before we were on the stands. So we were all fired, except John Nanovic, who was kept on to run* The Shadow. *. . . That year of 1933 was a desperate time. There was no chance of getting a newspaper job. The number of N.Y. papers had halved in the past few months. One of my duties had been the reading of short stories to fill the back of* The Shadow, *which used four shorts an issue to back up Walter Gibson's 60,000-word novel. I knew we had been searching desperately for a 1300-word story, and also a 1700-word one. We had been laid off at five o'clock on Friday. Monday at eleven in the morning, I laid a 1300-word story on John Nanovic's desk. He read it and sent through a voucher for thirteen bucks. At four I put a 1700-word story in the same spot, and by closing time had made thirty bucks, which had been my salary the week before. And here I had four more days in which to scrounge.*

JOHN PELLEW: *I went to work in Street & Smith's art department in 1927. I was a bull pen worker doing layouts, pasteups, etc. From that I graduated to hand lettering chapter or story titles. Then to doing some pen and ink and drybrush illustration, mostly for* Sea Stories *magazine. An elderly man called Hines was art director. He had worked with N.C. Wyeth and all the old timers. My first art directing job was to read part of a story to Mr. Hines and suggest an illustrator for it. As a rule he fell asleep before I had finished so I was on my own. He always approved the final illustration anyway.*

BRUNO FISCHER: *In the spring of 1936 I was editor of the Socialist Call, the official weekly of the Socialist Party. I'd got married two years before . . . and the way radical publications paid in those days of depression our primary income came from my wife's job. One afternoon while brooding in a bar (rye—two drinks for a quarter)* *with one of my editors over how to make a living while editing, he mentioned that for a while he had written pulp stories. I'd never read one, but on the way home, rather high, I bought a number. Several were what the trade called horror-terror magazines. It seemed to me that they would be most up my alley since they required style and mood and atmosphere, and I was nothing if not a competent writer. I spent the week writing a Poe-type short of 6,000 words and sent it out to Popular Publications, which was the leading house for that kind of magazine. A couple of weeks later I got my first letter from Rogers Terrill with a check for sixty dollars. In those days that was quite a sum. I then wrote a 10,000-word novelette and got a check for $125—a raise to 1½¢ a word. By the end of the year I had earned $2,000 on horror-terror shorts. I quit my job and it was almost twenty-five years before I did anything but write free-lance.*

WILLIAM KOFOED: *In 1928, I tried to sell George Delacorte on the idea of publishing a pulp called* Fight Stories. *He thought the market too limited, so I took it up to Jack Kelly, co-owner with Jack Glenister of Fiction House. Both Kelly and Glenister had been circulation men, originally "road men," then managers. Kelly had already rented a small office on Eighth Avenue down near Penn Station, when one day he ran into Jack Glenister on Madison Avenue, told him of his plans and suggested a partnership. So the two Jacks became publishers, Kelly the editor, Glenister the business and circulation manager. They also swabbed up their office nightly to save the cost of a cleaning woman.* Action Stories *was their first pulp. . . . When Lindbergh flew the Atlantic, Kelly knew the next natural title for a pulp was* Air Stories, *which he promptly added to his growing chain, then,* Wings. *Both these magazines along with the now well established* Action Stories *made both men rich. Kelly was a fight fan, so he went for my* Fight Stories

*right off. I wanted part ownership, which he would not
grant. So he gave me a salary bigger than any of the other
editors . . . I was also supposed to be cut in on the profits,
but that didn't materialize.*

KEN CROSSEN: *How did I become an editor of* Detective Fiction Weekly? *I was a professional writer when I
was sixteen. I quit when I was nineteen. After doing a
number of different things, I left the Middle West and
went to New York City in 1935. I went to work on the
WPA Writers' Project as the Cricket Expert on the New
York City Guide Book. I was married in 1936 and an-
swered an advertisement for a job. I was hired to work on*
Detective Fiction Weekly. *The Munsey company was an
interesting place when I went to work there. Although
Frank Munsey was dead it was run in much the same
fashion that he had. Maybe not quite as eccentrically as
he had, since he was known for evaluating the worth of
a manuscript by how heavy it felt on his hand. We had
complete autonomy and any of our regular writers could
come in and get a cash draw against a story. All that had
to be done was the editor went in and signed a voucher,
received the money in cash and turned it over to the
writer. This applied to such writers as Richard Sale, Cor-
nell Woolrich, Judson Phillips, Borden Chase, Norbert
Davis, etc.*

ROBERT G. HARRIS: *In 1931, I went to New York for
further study in illustration, and fortunately came under the world's two greatest instructors: Harvey Dunn at
the Grand Central School of Art, and George Bridgeman
at the Art Student's League. . . . Somewhere along about
this time—and how it came about exactly I don't know
—all of us students were continually talking about how
to break into the illustration field, and continually I
would hear about the Pulps being a starting point for
illustration. . . . Looking the magazine stands over one
day, I decided that I could make my try in the Western*

Pulps. I was a Missouri boy who had sat a saddle and traveled many times to the far west with my father, who dearly loved the lore and color of the wide open spaces. My first approach was, of course, to see Street & Smith, the King of the Pulps. It was very early in the morning when I eagerly arrived. I never had seen a publishing plant before, and the thrill of seeing all this mass production of magazines, with the clatter and din of press, binding machines, and the over-all glorious smell of printers ink was a bit of heaven to me. Unfortunately, this morning the Art Director was not in so I decided, instead of waiting, to call on some other western pulp publication. My next call was at Thrilling Publications and whether it was my hat and boots, or they were desperate for art, I'll never know, but I was ushered in immediately.

FREDERICK C. DAVIS: *In '24 I entered Dartmouth College. In my second semester I had a scholarship, which was a help, but it wasn't nearly enough. So I had to make it on my own by writing for the pulps. I wrote a short story every week, starting a story on a Sunday, working on it a little every day during the week, copying it and sending it off on Saturday—then the same thing the next week and the next. I sold a good percentage of these. At the same time I was chalking up a scholastic rating of 3.8. It goes almost without saying that I had very little social life while in college. I left Dartmouth in the middle of my sophomore year to get married. I was doing detective and Western shorts and doing very well at it—and then air stories. I wrote and sold many air stories although I had never been within reaching distance of an airplane and certainly had never seen any action at the front—World War I broke out when I was a freshman in high school— but it was easy enough to pick up the necessary technicalities from the magazines themselves. In 1930 or thereabouts I found myself back in Manhattan, and it was then that I began to develop a full head of steam.*

Before long my output was 125,000 words a month. I kept up this pace month after month for years, with hardly a vacation.... What did I know about the pulp audience? The best of the pulp magazines were aimed at adults, but of course I knew most of them were for juveniles. I was concerned with the reader only indirectly. The reader was the editor's business. My business was the editor.

ROBERT SIDNEY BOWEN: *Yes, I ghosted a mess of the prominent house characters, and many times. Such as Phantom Detective, the Lone Eagle, Captain Danger, and so forth. I have them all listed in my records, but unfortunately I recorded them under the initials of the magazine instead of the full name, and today I can't for the life of me remember what some of those initials stand for. As an example, I see by my records that I wrote the lead novel in eight different issues of a magazine I've recorded as M.F., but what M.F. stands for I haven't the faintest idea. When I started writing fiction full time I wrote about seven hours a day, seven days a week. And countless, countless times I've written all night to get a rush job done in time. Back in those days when I was writing nothing but pulp stuff I averaged about a hundred and fifty-odd short stories and novelets a year. And my yearly wordage averaged four or five hundred thousand words.*

MERLE CONSTINER: *I was born here in the village of Monroe, Ohio, but lived much of my life elsewhere. I have a Master's from Vanderbilt, where I minored in Medieval History, to show you how far you can wander in this vale of uncertainties. I went full time at writing about '38. I wasn't a racehorse producer, and still write slowly and painstakingly. No writers ever helped me, blast it. In my early days it was a solitary sort of kitchen table profession.*

RICHARD DEMING: *Was drafted March, 1941, nearly a year before W.W.II, spent 4¾ years in service (Army) and came out a captain. First pulp sale was a Manville*

Moon story titled The Juarez Knife, *bought by* Popular Detective *in Dec., 1945, but not published until the January, 1948, edition. Subsequently Manny Moon appeared in numerous pulp magazines, but mainly in* Black Mask *. . . . I think I once counted fifty-five different pulp magazines I had appeared in. . . . I did not see the complete end of the pulps coming as quickly as it did, and neither did most of the editors in the field. (Although all of us could see them dying.) In 1950 I decided to try full-time writing. At the time I was living about 500 miles from New York City. I had my agent arrange interviews with a half dozen of the pulp editors to whom I had been regularly selling, and went to New York for a few days. I came away with sufficient assignments to bring me an estimated eight hundred dollars a month just from pulp writing—not a bad income at that time. On November 1, 1950, I resigned my job. On November 7, the editor of* Black Mask *was fired without advance notice . . . By the end of November, every editor I had talked to in New York was out of a job, and the pulps were dead except for a few marginal ½¢-a-word things that hung on for a while. I made $1200 during the next twelve months.*

HOWARD BROWNE: *At the age of seventeen, I hitchhiked to Chicago to see my first major-league ballgame. Instead of staying in the city for a weekend, as planned, I hung around for the next twenty-six years. At the age of thirty, married and one child, I decided to get out of my job as credit manager for a furniture chain, and into the writing business. . . . I wrote two pulp detective stories, sent them to Ziff-Davis, which bought them both; and on taking the second one, they hired me to edit their detective magazine. . . . From 1942, when I started at Z-D, till 1947, when I took a two-year sabbatical in California to write three novels, I wrote two novels and God knows how many pulp stories under more pennames than I'll ever remember. In 1949, Ray Palmer left Z-D and I came* *back as editor-in-chief of the Fiction Group. In 1950, the entire company moved from Chicago to New York. . . . Actually, science fiction bored the beJesus out of me— although I've always enjoyed good fantasy. I've written my share of both—most of it highly forgetable. In 1950, I talked the Z-D brass into going digest size on both* Amazing *and* Fantastic. *I raised the rates to as much as ten cents a word, and used two-color interior art work. Both books at first were critical successes; but TV was already beginning to erode the pulp market . . . It all seems long ago and far away.*